Money, Finance, and Capitalist Crisis

T0300179

Extraordinary growth of the financial relative to the nonfinancial sector has marked the development of mature capitalism during the last four decades. The changing balance between the two sectors has altered the outlook of the economy and facilitated the spread of financial concerns, practices, and outlooks across society. The result has been the gradual transformation of contemporary capitalism – namely, its financialization since the late 1970s.

There are similarities between the Marxist, the Post-Keynesian and other heterodox approaches to analyzing the profound changes in money and finance in the global economy since the 1980s. Prominent among them is a common focus on financialization but also on the limits of monetary policy, the transformation of banking, the tendency to crisis related to financial excess, and the problematic role of neoliberalism in finance. Furthermore, the complexity of the interrelationship between finance and the rest of the economy has increased since the great crisis of 2007–9. This book tackles several of these developments as well as engaging in debate among different currents of heterodox economics.

The chapters of the book were originally published as articles in *The Japanese Political Economy*.

Nobuharu Yokokawa is Professor of Economics, Musashi University, Tokyo. He is Editor-in-Chief of *The Japanese Political Economy* and has published widely on the topics of political economy, evolutionary economics, economic history and development economics.

Costas Lapavitsas is Professor of Economics at the School of Oriental and African Studies, University of London. He is internationally known and has published widely on money and finance, contemporary capitalism, the Eurozone, and other topics.

Money, Finance, and Capitalist Crisis

Edited by
Nobuharu Yokokawa and Costas Lapavitsas

Routledge
Taylor & Francis Group

LONDON AND NEW YORK

First published 2022
by Routledge
4 Park Square, Milton Park, Abingdon, Oxon, OX14 4RN

and by Routledge
605 Third Avenue, New York, NY 10158

Routledge is an imprint of the Taylor & Francis Group, an informa business

© 2022 Taylor & Francis

British Library Cataloguing in Publication Data
A catalogue record for this book is available from the British Library

ISBN: 978-1-032-24934-6 (hbk)
ISBN: 978-1-032-24936-0 (pbk)
ISBN: 978-1-003-28082-8 (ebk)

DOI: 10.4324/9781003280828

Typeset in Minion Pro
by Newgen Publishing UK

Publisher's Note
The publisher accepts responsibility for any inconsistencies that may have arisen during the conversion of this book from journal articles to book chapters, namely the inclusion of journal terminology.

Disclaimer
Every effort has been made to contact copyright holders for their permission to reprint material in this book. The publishers would be grateful to hear from any copyright holder who is not here acknowledged and will undertake to rectify any errors or omissions in future editions of this book.

Contents

Citation Information

The chapters in this book, except chapter 6, were originally published in *The Japanese Political Economy*, volume 45, issue 1–2 (2019). Chapter 6 was originally published in volume 46, issue 1 (2020) of the same journal. When citing this material, please use the original citations and page numbering for each article, as follows:

Introduction
    Introduction: Money, finance, and capitalist crisis
    Nobuharu Yokokawa and Costas Lapavitsas
    The Japanese Political Economy, volume 45, issue 1–2 (2019), pp. 1–3

Chapter 1
    Profitability trends in the era of financialization: Notes on the U.S. economy
    Costas Lapavitsas and Ivan Mendieta-Muñoz
    The Japanese Political Economy, volume 45, issue 1–2 (2019), pp. 4–19

Chapter 2
    The comparative advantage of the U.S. shadow banking system and the role of the U.S. dollar
    Junji Tokunaga
    The Japanese Political Economy, volume 45, issue 1–2 (2019), pp. 20–42

Chapter 3
    Building blocks for the macroeconomics and political economy of housing
    Engelbert Stockhammer and Christina Wolf
    The Japanese Political Economy, volume 45, issue 1–2 (2019), pp. 43–67

Chapter 4
    Marx's Financial Capitalism
    Makoto Nishibe
    The Japanese Political Economy, volume 45, issue 1–2 (2019), pp. 68–80

Chapter 5

Financialization and the impasse of capitalism
François Chesnais
The Japanese Political Economy, volume 45, issue 1–2 (2019), pp. 81–103

Chapter 6

State involvement in cryptocurrencies. A potential world money?
Juan J. Duque
The Japanese Political Economy, volume 46, issue 1 (2020), pp. 65–82

For any permission-related enquiries please visit:
www.tandfonline.com/page/help/permissions

Notes on Contributors

François Chesnais, Universite Paris-Nord, Paris, France.

Juan J. Duque, Department of Economics, SOAS, University of London, London, UK.

Costas Lapavitsas, Department of Economics, SOAS University of London, London, UK.

Ivan Mendieta-Muñoz, Department of Economics, University of Utah, Salt Lake City, Utah, USA.

Makoto Nishibe, Department of Economics, Senshu University, Kawasaki, Japan.

Engelbert Stockhammer, Department of International Political Economy, King's College, London, UK.

Junji Tokunaga, Economic Department, Dokkyo University, Saitama, Japan.

Christina Wolf, Department of Economics, Kingston University, London, UK.

Nobuharu Yokokawa, Musashi University, Tokyo, Japan.

Introduction: Money, finance, and capitalist crisis

Nobuharu Yokokawa and Costas Lapavitsas (ID)

Extraordinary growth of the financial relative to the nonfinancial sector has marked the development of mature capitalism during the last four decades. The changing balance between the two sectors has altered the outlook of the economy and facilitated the spread of financial concerns, practices, and outlook across society. The result has been the gradual transformation of contemporary capitalism—namely, its financialization since the late 1970s. Financialization is marked by three profound tendencies: first, reduced reliance of nonfinancial enterprises on borrowed funds for investment; second, turning of banks toward transacting in open markets and household lending; and, third, increasing involvement of households in formal finance. These tendencies are summed up in the extraction of financial profit by various agents.

We believe that there are similarities between the Marxian, the Post-Keynesian and other heterodox approaches to analyzing the profound changes in money and finance in the global economy since the 1980s. Prominent among them is a common focus on financialization but also on the limits of monetary policy, the transformation of banking, the tendency to crisis related to financial excess, and the problematic role of neoliberalism in finance. Furthermore, the complexity of the interrelationship between finance and the rest of the economy has increased since the great crisis of 2007-9. This special issue of JPE provides an opportunity to tackle some of these developments as well as engaging in debate among different currents of heterodox economics.

The paper by Costas Lapavitsas and Ivan Mendieta-Muñoz, titled "Profitability trends in the era of financialization: Notes on the U.S. economy" considers the evolution of financialization of the US economy by examining the profitability and the volume of profits of the financial sector relative to general profitability and total profits in the economy. It is shown that financial profitability rose strongly from the early 1980s to the early 2000s. Similarly, the volume of financial profits reached extraordinary levels in the early 2000s. The authors argue that the great crisis of 2007–9 acted as a threshold point beyond which both the profitability and the volume of profits of the financial sector have not recovered previous levels.

Junji Tokunaga in his paper titled "The Comparative Advantage of the U.S. Shadow Banking System and the Role of the U.S. Dollar" examines the factors that enabled European banks to expand their USD-denominated balance sheets across the Atlantic through the U.S. shadow banking system in the 2000s. He argues that the comparative advantage of U.S. shadow banking system relative to the less advanced system in the Eurozone allowed European banks to expand USD-denominated balance sheets across the Atlantic, resulting in the reign of the U.S. dollar in the shadow banking system in the 2000s. He concludes that strong demand for long-term private U.S. debt securities and short-term U.S. financial instruments contributed to the reign of the U.S. dollar in the shadow banking system. The U.S. dollar standard system remained as asymmetric as ever in the 2000s.

Engelbert Stockhammer and Christina Wolf in their paper "Building blocks for the macroeconomics and political economy of housing" examine the role of housing in the global financial crisis 2007–08 and the Euro crisis. They survey different theoretical approaches to housing: mainstream economics, Post-Keynesian theory, Comparative Political Economy, and Marxist political economy. They emphasize the importance of adopting a class- and rent-based approach to housing, empirically based on the link with political attitudes and macroeconomic dynamics. They also investigate empirical aspects of housing in the UK from a class-analytic perspective.

Makoto Nishibe, in his paper "Marx's Financial Capitalism" argues that "financialization" is one aspect of the "free investment capitalism." He identifies several stages of market domination of the real economy. The capitalist economy was established with the general commodification of goods and the external commodification of labor power. Nishibe proposes the application of the concept of fictitious capital to human labour as a means of analysing the financialization of household income through loans and the accumulation of financial assets. He further distinguishes three stages of the capitalist economy with regard to the mode of commodification of labour power: E(external) Mode; I(internal) Mode; and G(general) Mode. He argues that in G mode (capitalist market economy with general commodification of labor power) labor power becomes a capitalistic product aiming at profit, and it is then transformed into fictitious capital (human capital). Globalization is ultimately oriented toward "free investment capitalism" where people, goods, and money move globally in search of high profitability.

François Chesnais in his paper titled "Financialization and the impasse of capitalism" argues that the decisive characteristic of financialization is the preeminence of financial accumulation over productive accumulation and of capital-as-property over capital-as-function. He examines the importance of inter-corporate power relationships in the distribution of surplus value, and contemporary banking and the sources of financial profits.

Finally, we have also included a paper by Juan Duque in this collection, titled "State involvement in cryptocurrencies. A potential world money?". The paper was not part of the original special issue but it was published in The Japanese Political Economy, 46(1). We have included it because we believe that it is a significant contribution to the unfolding debate on cryptocurrencies as new forms of money and complements the rest of the articles in the best possible way.

Duque offers an innovative analysis of cryptocurrencies as a pure form of what Marx identified as the peculiar use-value of money, namely the ability to buy. Distributed ledger technology has created the possibility for this use-value to emerge digitally. Duque takes an important step in exploring the implications of this development for contemporary capitalism by considering the actions of central banks. If cryptocurrencies are going to challenge credit money as the dominant form of money in the future, it follows that potential role as world money is likely to be a pivotal element. The impact on hegemony in the world market could be decisive. Duque's contribution opens a early path for Marxist economics to begin to consider the likely implications for contemporary capitalism.

We hope that this special feature will contribute to a critical assessment of financialization, initiating further debate among different currents of heterodox economics.

ORCID

Costas Lapavitsas (iD) http://orcid.org/0000-0001-9330-7105

Profitability trends in the era of financialization: Notes on the U.S. economy

Costas Lapavitsas and Ivan Mendieta-Muñoz

ABSTRACT
This article considers the evolution of financialization in the U.S. economy by examining the profitability and the volume of profits of the financial sector relative to general profitability and total profits in the economy. It is shown that financial profitability rose strongly from the early 1980s to the early 2000s. Similarly, the volume of financial profits reached extraordinary levels in the early 2000s. These phenomena occurred while interest rates and the net interest margin of banks were on a downward trend and, broadly speaking, reflect financial expropriation in the U.S. economy. The great crisis of 2007–2009 has acted as a threshold point beyond which both the profitability and the volume of profits of the financial sector have not recovered to previous levels. It is possible, but not certain, that a rebalancing of the productive and the financial sectors is under way in the financialized U.S. economy.

Introduction: Profitability trends in the course of financialization

Extraordinary growth of the financial relative to the nonfinancial sector has marked the development of mature capitalism during the last four decades. The changing balance between the two sectors has altered the outlook of the economy and facilitated the spread of financial concerns, practices, and outlook across society. The result has been the gradual transformation of contemporary capitalism—namely, its financialization since the late 1970s.[1]

Within the framework of Marxist political economy, and following Lapavitsas (2013), financialization can be characterized as the outcome of three underlying tendencies: first, reduced reliance of nonfinancial enterprises on borrowed funds for investment; second, turning of banks toward transacting in open markets and household lending; and, third, increasing involvement of households in formal finance. These tendencies are summed up in the extraction of financial profit by various agents within the economy. It follows that an important analytical approach to characterizing financialization as a historical period is to examine the trajectory of the relevant profitability measures during the last several decades. After all, capitalism rests on the making of profit, and thus the trajectory and fluctuations of financial profit are crucial to the analysis of financialization, as is also the relationship between financial and total profit over time.

It is reasonable to expect, *a priori*, that during the period of financialization both financial profitability and the proportion of financial profit have increased relative to general profitability and total profit. With this expectation in mind, the relationship between financial and total profit in the U.S. economy is discussed in the rest of the article by considering various measures of aggregate profitability during the period 1955–2015. The analysis deploys publicly available data obtained from Duménil and Lévy (2016), the Federal Deposit Insurance Corporation (FDIC), the Federal Reserve Bank of St. Louis (FRED), and the National Income and Product Accounts (NIPA) published by U.S. Bureau of Economic Analysis (BEA).

A major difficulty in this respect is that financial profit is a difficult concept to define theoretically. Broadly speaking, it can be taken to refer to profit made through financial transactions by a range of economic agents, and not only by capitalists (Lapavitsas 2013). Furthermore, in line with standard Marxist political economy, financial profit can be considered to derive principally as a share of the flow of total profit (surplus value) generated by the nonfinancial sector. It has become apparent in the years of financialization, however, that financial profit can also derive out of the flows of personal income as well as from the redivision of money holdings across society (mostly as various forms of capital gains). Precisely for this reason, financial profit has given rise to the concept of "financial expropriation," that is, profit deriving via expropriating methods from the income and wealth of others. In short, financial expropriation is characteristic of financialization and captures profits arising out of transfers of household income but also of money wealth, chiefly in the form of capital gains (Lapavitsas 2009, 2013).

Unfortunately, it is extremely difficult to measure financial profit by deploying national income accounts or other publicly available macroeconomic statistics, when such profit is defined in the appropriate "envelope" terms outlined above. For one thing, there is no clearly established way of measuring financial profit that arises out of capital gains. Given this difficulty, and despite the undoubted importance of capital gains and other forms of financial expropriation in the course of financialization, the best way of empirically approximating financial profit is simply to measure the profits of financial institutions, above all, of commercial banks.

After measuring financial profit, the main problem is to establish its relationship to total profit. There are two methods of pursuing this task, both of which are standard in Marxist political economy. The first is to compare the rate of financial profit to the general rate of profit; the second is to compare the volume (or mass) of financial relative to total profit. Each method could cast a different light on the path and the direction of financialized mature capitalism in the United States. The comparisons, furthermore, would broadly reflect the balance between the financial and the nonfinancial sections of the U.S. capitalist class.

Empirical analysis in the following sections examines the relationship between financial and total profit in the U.S. economy during the period 1955–2015 by deploying both methods. On this basis, conclusions are drawn about the trajectory of the U.S. financialization. The fundamental reason for focusing exclusively on the United States is the availability of data, which is by far the best among developed countries. At the same time, the United States is the paradigmatic country of financialization, and thus the conclusions reached about the U.S. economy may have a broader significance for financialization elsewhere. Nonetheless, it is vital to acknowledge at the outset the data limitations in tackling the complex research question of this article. The results presented below should be taken *cum grano salis*.

Comparing the general rate of profit to the rate of profit of commercial banks

The main purpose of this section is to compare the rate of financial profit to the general rate of profit. To the best of our knowledge, this is the first time such a comparison has been attempted for the U.S. economy, and the evidence presented is new. The results offer a fresh and penetrating insight into the trajectory of U.S. financialization that could also facilitate further analysis for other countries.

Estimating the relevant profit rates is a complex task. There is an enormous Marxist literature on the general rate of profit, including its trajectory in the long and the short term. We have deployed a simple measure of the general rate of profit for the U.S. economy obtained from the dataset provided by Duménil and Lévy (2016). Moreover, there are tremendous conceptual difficulties with regard to financial profit arising from its inchoate and "envelope" character. Put simply, there cannot be a general rate of return that reflects at once the profitability of banks, the rate of financial profits made by nonfinancial enterprises, the profitability of pension funds, the rate of profit made by individuals derived from financial assets, and so on. The fundamental reason is that such rates cannot achieve uniformity,

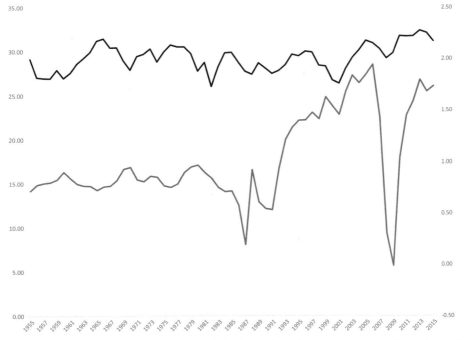

Figure 1. United States, 1955–2015 (annual data). Total profits as percentage of net domestic product (black line, left axis) and net operating income of commercial banks as a percentage of net domestic product (red line, right axis). Source: Our own elaboration using data obtained from Duménil and Lévy (DL; 2016) and the Federal Deposit Insurance Corporation (FDIC). (Total profits: net domestic product minus wages, DL; net domestic product: DL; financial profits: pre-tax net operating income for commercial banks, FDIC, Table CB04. Net income for all insured commercial banks.)

as they are not all earned by competing capitals, and thus do not reflect the movement of resources across different areas of the economy. There is no general rate of financial profit that is formed in a manner analogous to the general rate of profit. In this light, a useful proxy for financial profits is the net operating income of commercial banks, which are the pivot of the financial system. Data for that is available from the FDIC online database.

Given this proxy for financial profit, the first step is to establish an initial proportionate relation between financial and total profit in the U.S. economy. A simple way of doing that is to standardize both forms of profit with regard to gross domestic product (GDP). The ratios would obviously not reflect pure measures of profitability but nonetheless offer insight into the relative weight of each form of profit in the U.S. economy in the course of financialization. Furthermore, note that Duménil and Lévy (2016) have sought the broadest definition of profitability by calculating the annual volume of total profits in relation to net domestic product (NDP). It is expedient to follow the same path using NDP to standardize profit measures.

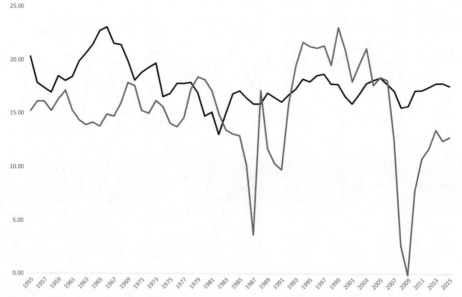

Figure 2. United States, 1955–2015 (annual data). Rate of profit (black line) and rate of profit of commercial banks (red line), in percentages. Source: Our own elaboration using data obtained from Duménil and Lévy (DL; 2016) and the Federal Deposit Insurance Corporation (FDIC). (Rate of profit: total profits [net domestic product minus wages, DL] divided by net stock of fixed capital [DL]; rate of profit of commercial banks: pretax net operating income for commercial banks [FDIC, Table CB04. net income for all insured commercial banks] divided by total equity capital [FDIC, Table CB14. liabilities and equity capital.])

Figure 1 plots the respective ratios of financial and nonfinancial (total) profit to NDP in the U.S. economy. Several important points are apparent from visual inspection alone:

1. Nonfinancial profits have exhibited a slight upward trend relative to NDP during the period following the Second World War.
2. Financial profits began to rise steadily relative to NDP after the middle of the 1980s, and peaked in 2006.
3. Financial profits collapsed relative to NDP in the course of the great crisis of 2007–2009, but rebounded strongly soon afterward, although they have not regained an upward trend.

In sum, the relative weight of financial profit in the U.S. economy rose steadily in the course of financialization. However, the balance between the two forms of profit appears to have shifted since the great crisis of 2007–2009. The preliminary evidence seems to suggest that the crisis has acted as a threshold point dampening the historic upward trajectory of financial profits.

The ratios of profit volumes relative to NDP are informative, but a far a more accurate view of the balance between the two sectors of the economy can be obtained by establishing the relevant rates of profit. The general rate of profit can be extracted from the dataset provided by Duménil and Lévy (2016). For the financial sector, on the other hand, suffice it to measure the rate of profit of commercial banks, which can be approximated by estimating the net operating income of banks as a percentage of their total equity capital. Thus, Figure 2 shows the general rate of profit compared to the rate of profit of commercial banks for the U.S. economy. Comparing the two rates is not common in the literature on financialization, but is revealing about the characteristics of the period.

The general rate of profit declined steadily and precipitously from the mid-1960s to the early 1980s, at which time the decline stopped and the estimated rate even began to rise gently over time. The rate of profit of commercial banks, on the other hand, rose strongly from the end of the Second World War to the late 1950s, after which it fluctuated at broadly the same level until the early 1980s. Bank profitability declined sharply in the early 1980s and collapsed during the stock market crash of 1987. After that event, however, U.S. banking entered a period of exceptional profitability that lasted (with fluctuations) until the first years of the 2000s. Bank profitability again declined precipitously in the great crisis of 2007–2009 but rebounded strongly afterwards, although without recovering an upward trend. The period lasting broadly from the mid-1980s to the mid-2000s appears to be the golden era of financialization, as far as commercial bank profitability is concerned.

The factors that determine the profitability of commercial banks are not well established in theory, in contrast to general profitability on which there is a vast literature.[2] It seems sensible to postulate that the profitability of commercial banks depends on the margin of interest income earned on their interest earning assets, plus the difference between noninterest income and expenditure.[3] Even without a widely accepted theory, however, it is clear that bank profitability depends on the rate of interest, which is likely to affect the interest margin of banks, and perhaps even their noninterest earnings and costs. Thus, the trajectory of the rate of interest is a vital part of the comparison of financial to total profit.

The benchmark rate of interest selected in this article is the federal funds real interest rate—that is, the nominal federal funds rate adjusted for the rate of inflation. This is the key reference rate for the entire structure of interest rates in the U.S. economy and reflects the stance of the U.S. central bank. It is a public rate of interest that depends on the creditworthiness of the Federal Reserve—and therefore, of the U.S. state—in the financial markets. There is no doubt that this rate of interest has emerged as the pivotal price of the financial system in the course of financialization. Crucial to this development has been the ability of the U.S. central bank to

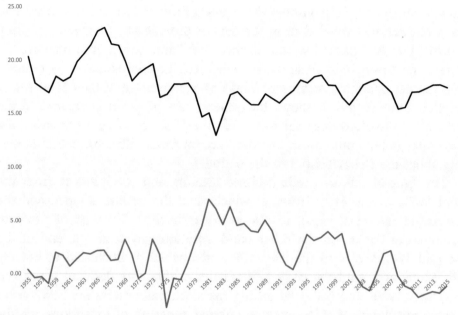

Figure 3. United States, 1955–2015 (annual data). Rate of profit (black line) and real rate of interest (red line), in percentages. Source: Our own elaboration using data obtained from Duménil and Lévy (DL; 2016) and the Federal Reserve Bank of St. Louis (FRED). (Rate of profit: total profits [net domestic product minus wages, DL] divided by net stock of fixed capital [DL]; real rate of interest: effective federal funds rate [FRED, FEDFUNDS series] minus inflation rate calculated using the net domestic product deflator [DL]).

manipulate the provision of liquidity to the U.S. economy through its command over inconvertible fiat money. The collapse of the Bretton Woods Agreement in 1971–1973, which led to the abolition of the convertibility of the U.S. dollar into gold at a fixed price, was an historic event that laid the ground for financialization.

The relation between historically low real interest rates and profitability in the course of financialization is of considerable interest. Figure 3 allows for a preliminary discussion by showing the trend of, respectively, the general rate of profit and the real federal funds rate.

The trajectory of the real interest rate offers significant insight with regard to financial profit. The rate peaked in the early 1980s as a result of the "Volcker Shock"—the extraordinary increase in nominal rates by the Federal Reserve with the aim of controlling inflation. However, since that time the real federal funds rate has been on a declining trend. The period of exceptionally high bank profitability shown in Figure 2 coincided with generally declining real interest rates. Indeed, it is striking that since the crisis of 2007–2009, the real federal funds rate has been systematically in negative territory. In effect, the public rate of interest has been pushed down, and even made negative, mostly through control over contemporary

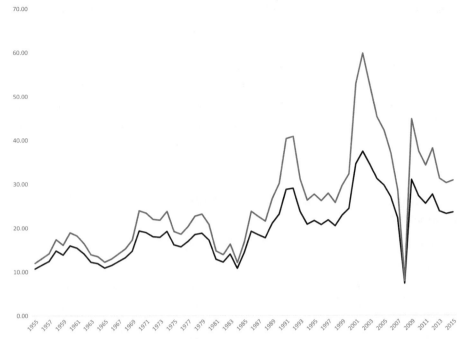

Figure 4. United States, 1955–2015 (annual data). Financial profits as percentage of corporate profits of domestic industries (black line) and financial profits as percentage of nonfinancial corporate profits (red line). Source: Our own elaboration using data obtained from the National Income and Product Accounts (NIPA), Bureau of Economic Analysis (BEA). (Financial profits; corporate profits of domestic industries; nonfinancial corporate profits: NIPA, BEA, Table 6.16. Corporate profits by industry [with inventory valuation and capital consumption adjustments]).

fiat money by the central bank. In this regard, financialization has certainly not been an era of the traditional *rentier*—that is, of the owner of money capital who makes returns out of lending and benefits from high interest rates.

Moreover, the gap between the general profit rate and the real federal funds rate is a useful proxy for the space available to nonfinancial capitalists to earn returns. Specifically, the gap is an indication of the scope for nonfinancial capitalists to earn what Hilferding called "profit of enterprise" on their investments.[4] It is clear that the gap narrowed steadily from the mid-1950 to the early 1980s because the general profit rate fell while the real federal funds rate rose dramatically in the late 1970s. The years of financialization have, however, witnessed the steady reopening of the gap mostly because the real rate of interest has tended to fall. This phenomenon has been partly due to state manipulation of interest rates throughout the period of financialization.

Remarkably, Figure 3 indicates that the period of financialization, despite the extraordinary prominence of financial profits, has brought a steady expansion of the scope for "profit of enterprise" compared to its constriction in previous decades. Indeed, since the crisis of 2007–2009, the gap between the curves has attained nearly the magnitude it had in the 1960s, the high time of the long boom following the Second World War. This aspect of financialization is potentially of considerable importance for the future development of U.S. capitalism and requires further examination. For that, however, it is necessary to consider in more detail the trajectory of the volumes of financial and total profits.

Comparing the volume of financial relative to total profit in the U.S. economy

Comparing the volume (or mass) of financial profit relative to the volume of total profit in the U.S. economy during the period of financialization can cast further light on the issue of relative profitability. To this purpose there is already considerable work on which to draw, including Lapavitsas and Mendieta-Muñoz (2016, 2017, 2018).

Consider the evidence presented in Figure 4, which is based on official data (obtained from NIPA) and shows financial profit as a percentage, first, of corporate profit of domestic industries and, second, of nonfinancial corporate profits.

Broadly speaking, the volume of financial relative to domestic profit in the U.S. economy fluctuated in the range of 10 to 20 percent from the middle of the 1950s to the beginning of the 1980s. The ensuing two decades, from the early 1980s to the early 2000s, were perhaps the golden era of financialization. The proportion of financial profit relative to corporate profit of domestic industries (the black line) reached extraordinary levels in the early 2002, in the region of 40 percent. However, the crisis of 2007–2009 witnessed a sharp collapse of financial profit. The recovery was equally pronounced, but the proportion of financial profit did not return to previous heights and has been even drifting downward. As discussed by Lapavitsas and Mendieta-Muñoz (2018), the crisis represents a structural break in the series and signals a different period in the trajectory of financialization lasting to the present day. Similar conclusions follow from comparing the volume of financial profit to the volume of nonfinancial corporate profit in the United States.

In sum, Figure 4 indicates that the balance between the financial and the nonfinancial sections of the U.S. capitalist class changed significantly in the course of financialization, shifting in favor of the former. However, the golden era appears to have come to an end in the early 2000s, and although financial profit has continued to be a very high proportion of total profit, the great crisis of 2007–2009 can be considered as a threshold point.[5]

In the extant literature there is little theoretical analysis of the proportionate weight of financial profits in the U.S. economy. However, recent work—mainstream as well as Marxist and other heterodox—has made some progress in explaining both the trajectory and the determining factors of financial profits. Thus, DeYong and Rice (2004a, 2004b) have emphasized the importance of the interest margin (earned by banks by intermediating between depositors and borrowers) and of noninterest income (earned by banks by charging their customers fees for a variety of financial services). Greenwood and Scharfstein (2013), Malkiel (2013), and Philippon and Reshef (2013) have stressed the importance of fees deriving from asset management services and residential mortgages. Total fees charged professionally to manage the value of financial assets have grown dramatically (driven largely by an increase in stock market valuations). Household credit has also contributed to the income growth of the financial sector, mainly through fees on loan origination, underwriting of asset-backed securities, trading and management of fixed-income products, and derivatives trading.

More immediately relevant to our purposes is that Lapavitsas and Mendieta-Muñoz (2017), following a Marxist approach, have shown that the relative weight of financial profit depends on a range of factors: positively on the net interest margin and the noninterest income of banks, but negatively on the general rate of profit, the noninterest expenses of banks, and the ratio of the total capital stock to the interest-earning assets held by banks. By far the most important factors are the net interest margin and the noninterest income of banks, both of which are discussed in further detail in this section.

The net interest margin of banks is a useful concept that captures the fundamental intermediary function of banking in a capitalist economy. It is defined as the difference between the interest earned and the interest paid by banks divided by their interest-earning assets. Essentially, it reflects net interest income earned per unit of assets. The noninterest income of banks, on the other hand, captures the broader functioning of banking in a capitalist economy, including the provision of liquidity and other related services (money dealing) as well as income deriving from mediating transactions and other nonlending activities in which banks engage. Noninterest income by banks casts light on financialization and the role of banks in mediating transactions and earning fees and commissions, rather than lending.

Of considerable importance in this respect are also the noninterest expenses of banks, which capture the costs of buildings, equipment, and labor employed by banks in delivering their functions. These are net costs,

Figure 5. United States, 1955–2015 (annual data). Net interest margin for commercial banks, in percentage. Source: Our own elaboration using data obtained from the Federal Deposit Insurance Corporation (FDIC). (Net interest margin for commercial banks: Net Interest income [FDIC, Table CB04. Net Income] divided by total interest earning assets [FDIC, Table CB16. Interest Earning Assets and Interest Bearing Liabilities]).

a *faux frais*, of capitalist production, since they are not reproduced as a flow of value. They are a dead-weight loss for a capitalist economy, representing the social burden of having an integral financial system. Crucially for our purposes, the noninterest expenses of banks include salaries, wages, and bonuses. Thus, they include a part of financial profit that appears as a cost and is hard to measure comprehensively in the aggregate.

In this light, consider Figures 5 and 6, which show the net interest margin and the noninterest income and expenditure of U.S. commercial banks. It is immediately apparent that the golden era of financialization in the United States was characterized by a remarkable increase in the net interest margin, followed by an even more remarkable decline. The peak occurred in the early 1990s, and the steepest collapse in the early 2000s. To the best of our knowledge, there is no coherent theory that explains the behavior of the net interest margin of banks. It stands to reason, however, that the net interest margin is related to the differential sensitivity of bank assets and liabilities to the interest rate as well as to the ability of banks to vary interest rates differentially across the balance sheet. It is plausible, for instance, that interest rates on loans could be changed less flexibly than interest rates on deposits.

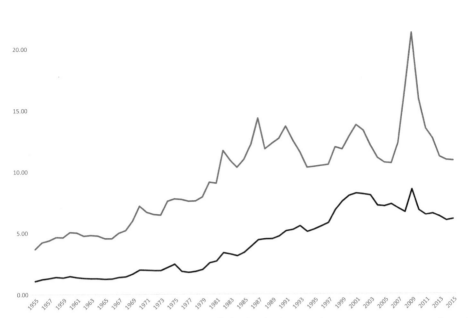

Figure 6. United States, 1955–2015 (annual data). Noninterest income as percentage of total profits (black line) and noninterest expense as percentage of total profits (red line). Source: Our own elaboration using data obtained from the Federal Deposit Insurance Corporation (FDIC) and Duménil and Lévy (DL; 2016). (Noninterest income: total noninterest income for commercial banks, FDIC, Table CB04. Net income; noninterest expense: total noninterest expense plus provision for loan and lease losses, FDIC, Table CB04. Net income; total profits: net domestic product minus wages, DL.)

Figure 5 shows clearly that bank profits came under increasing pressure from interest rates after the early 1990s. The extraordinary peak in the volume of financial profits in the early 2000s coincided with low interest margins. Two points are immediately apparent from the diagram in this respect.

First, financialization hardly represents the return of the rentier, if the rentier is an agent (or a section of the capitalist class) that seeks to lend money capital on interest. Indeed, the second half of the golden era of financialization looks more like Keynes's "euthanasia of the rentier," in view of the collapse of the net interest margin. Second, the extraordinary profits of banks derived in good part from noninterest sources, which rose enormously in importance during the years of financialization. Financial expropriation resting on the ability of banks to extract profits through transactions, fees, and commissions is obliquely reflected in Figure 6. The trajectory of the curves casts some light on this aspect of financialization by capturing the proportion of noninterest income to financial profits and the volume of noninterest expenditure to financial profits.

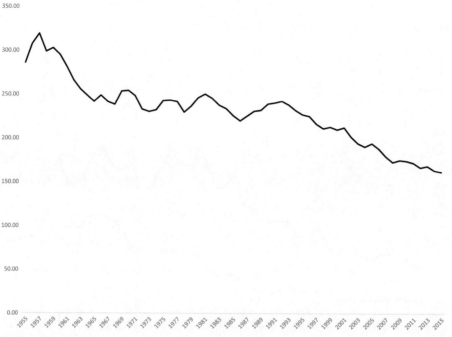

Figure 7. United States, 1955–2015 (annual data). Net stock of fixed capital as percentage of total interest earning assets. Source: Our own elaboration using data obtained from Duménil and Lévy (DL; 2016) and the Federal Deposit Insurance Corporation (FDIC). (Net stock of fixed capital: DL; total interest earning assets: FDIC, Table CB16. Interest Earning Assets and Interest Bearing Liabilities.)

Note that the noninterest income of banks began to rise very rapidly in the 2000s, precisely when the net interest margin came under heavy downward pressure. It is also important to note that the net interest margin surged back immediately after the crisis, only to decline rapidly again and subsequently to remain at low levels. At the same time, the noninterest income of banks stopped rising as rapidly as before and began to fluctuate at roughly the same level. On that note too, the great crisis of 2007–2009 appears to signal the end of the golden era of financialization.

Even more telling, finally, is the extraordinary growth in the noninterest expenditure of banks throughout the period of financialization, but most prominently after the 1990s. These greatly increased expenditures reflect the substantial cost represented by financialization for the economy as a whole. Financialization has not brought any noticeable improvement in the efficiency of the financial system, if that is measured by the dead-weight costs of finance. Philippon (2015) has discussed this weakness of contemporary finance by showing that the unit cost of financial intermediation has not decreased in the United States in recent decades, despite the advances in information technology and changes in the organization of the financial sector. Bazot (2018) found similar results for Germany, the United Kingdom, and more broadly for Europe, the only exception being France.

Given that noninterest expenditures conceal transfers of financial profits in the form of salaries, bonuses, and other forms of remuneration, the relative inefficiency of finance in the years of financialization probably reflects tremendous transfers of profits to the practitioners of finance, a form of financial rent accruing through occupying positions in the structures of finance and drawing on financial expropriation.

It is worth noting, finally, that the trajectory of financial profits before and after the crisis of 2007–2009 is only partly related to changes in aggregate indebtedness. Thus, when the latter is measured as the ratio of the total capital stock of the economy to the interest-earning assets of banks, Figure 7 shows that it declined gently after the crisis. The relative fall of indebtedness would have certainly affected the profits of banks, but on visual inspection alone it does not seem to be decisive.

Conclusion

Comparison of financial to total profits casts a revealing light on the evolution of financialization in the United States during the last four decades. The profitability of the financial sector witnessed a tremendous increase from the early 1980s to the early 2000s, the period that can be considered as the golden era of financialization. However, financial profitability has not regained the same levels since the late 2000s. The same conclusion follows by standardizing financial and total profit relative to NDP. Moreover, similar conclusions result by examining the volume (or mass) of financial and total profit in the course of financialization in the United States. From the early 1980s to the early 2000s, the volume of financial profits rose rapidly, reaching extraordinary levels in the early 2000s. Nevertheless, since the late 2000s financial profits have not regained an upward trend relative to total profits. Much of the rise and subsequent relative stagnation of financial profits has occurred while interest rates have been declining, as has the net interest margin of banks.

These characteristic features of financial profitability could well be the result of the shock delivered to bank operations by the great crisis of 2007–2009, and might indicate little more than the short-term adjustment of the financial sector to the conditions emerging after the crisis. But it is also possible that the crisis has acted as an historical threshold point, signifying the end of the golden era of financialization in the USA. A rebalancing between the financial and the nonfinancial sectors of the U.S. economy could well be under way. The evidence presented in this article certainly does not show a reversal of financialization in the United States, but it is possible that the high-water mark has passed. The implications would be profound and call for further analysis.

Notes

1. The literature on financialization has become enormous in recent years, and it is not the purpose of the present article to review it. Useful discussions can be found in Krippner (2005), Lapavitsas (2013), Lapavitsas and Mendieta-Muñoz (2018), and van der Zwan (2014).
2. For a general discussion of the rate of profit of banking capital relative to the general rate of profit, see Itoh and Lapavitsas (1999, Chapter 4).
3. In the next section, further insight into these factors is offered in connection with the volume of financial relative to the volume of total profit (but not between the respective rates of profit).
4. For a discussion of Hilferding's concept see Lapavitsas (2013).
5. It is crucial to remember, nonetheless, that the figures capture neither the financial profits made by the nonfinancial sector nor those deriving from capital gains, and should also be treated with caution.

References

Bazot, Guillaume. 2018. "Financial Consumption and the Cost of Finance: Measuring Financial Efficiency in Europe (1950-2007)." *Journal of the European Economic Association* 16 (1):123–60.

DeYong, Robert, and Tara Rice. 2004a. "How Do Banks Make Money? the Fallacies of Fee Income." *Federal Reserve Bank of Chicago Economic Perspectives* 4Q:34–51.

DeYong, Robert, and Tara Rice. 2004b. "Noninterest Income and Financial Performance at U.S. commercial Banks." *The Financial Review* 39 (1):101–27. doi: 10.1111/j.0732-8516.2004.00069.x.

Duménil, Gérard, and Dominique Lévy. 2016. "The Historical Trends of Technology and Distribution in the U.S. economy since 1869. Data and Figures." *Centre Pour la Reserche Économique et Ses Applications (CEPREMAP) Document.* Accessed February 10, 2019. http://www.cepremap.fr/membres/dlevy/dle2016e.pdf

Greenwood, Robin, and David Scharfstein. 2013. "The Growth of Finance." *Journal of Economic Perspectives* 27 (2):3–28. doi: 10.1257/jep.27.2.3.

Itoh, Makot, and Costas Lapavitsas. 1999. *Political Economy of Money and Finance.* London, UK: McMillan.

Krippner, Greta. 2005. "The Financialization of the American Economy." *Socio-Economic Review* 3 (2):173–208. doi: 10.1093/SER/mwi008.

Lapavitsas, Costas. 2009. "Financialized Capitalism: Crisis and Financial Expropriation." *Historical Materialism* 17 (2):114–48. doi: 10.1163/156920609X436153.

Lapavitsas, Costas. 2013. *Profiting without Producing: How Finance Exploits Us All.* London, UK: Verso.

Lapavitsas, Costas, and Ivan Mendieta-Muñoz. 2016. "The Profits of Financialization." *Monthly Review* 68 (3):49–62. doi: 10.14452/MR-068-03-2016-07_4.

Lapavitsas, Costas, and Ivan Mendieta-Muñoz. 2018. "Financialization at a Watershed in the USA." *Competition and Change* 22 (5):488–508. doi: 10.1177/1024529418769472.

Lapavitsas, Costas, and Ivan Mendieta-Muñoz. 2017. "Explaining the historic rise in financial profits in the US economy." Working Paper No. 2017-06, University of Utah, Department of Economics, Salt Lake City, Utah: USA: Working Paper Series.

Malkiel, Burton. 2013. "Asset Management Fees and the Growth of Finance." *Journal of Economic Perspectives* 27 (2):97–108. doi: 10.1257/jep.27.2.97.

Philippon, Thomas. 2015. "Has the US Finance Industry Become Less Efficient? On the Theory and Measurement of Financial Intermediation." *American Economic Review* 105 (4):1408–38. doi: 10.1257/aer.20120578.

Philippon, Thomas, and Ariell Reshef. 2013. "An International Look at the Growth of Modern Finance." *Journal of Economic Perspectives* 27 (2):73–96. doi: 10.1257/jep.27.2.73.

Van der Zwan, Natascha. 2014. "Making Sense of Financialization." *Socio-Economic Review* 12 (1):99–129. doi: 10.1093/ser/mwt020.

The comparative advantage of the U.S. shadow banking system and the role of the U.S. dollar

ABSTRACT

What facilitated European banks to expand their balance sheets denominated in the US dollar across the Atlantic through U.S. shadow banking system in the 2000s, despite the creation of the euro in 1999? In order to the question, this article argues that the European banks' balance sheets denominated in the dollar depended on the comparative advantage of the U.S. shadow banking system over one in the Eurozone in term of financial market side institutional side, resulting in the U.S. dollar reign in the shadow banking system in the 2000s. In conclusion, as far as the dominant position of the dollar in the shadow banking system, the U.S. dollar standard system has been as asymmetric as ever in the 2000s, rather than less asymmetric.

Introduction

European banks expanded their balance sheets significantly in the 2000s prior to the global financial crisis (GFC) of 2008. As has been acknowledged by many studies, the expansion of balance sheets by European banks in the 2000s was mainly due to five factors: (a) the generalized search for high returns in advanced countries, (b) the diversification of their portfolios geographically since the introduction of the euro, (d) the depreciation in U.S. dollar (USD) against the euro from mid-2001 onward, (c) the development of European financial integration, and (e) the benefit from inappropriately low capital requirements led by regulatory arbitrage under the Basel II.

Several studies have shed particular light on the last factor. Regulatory arbitrage under the Basel II risk-weight system allowed European banks to reduce their required regulatory capital ratio, allowing them to expand their balance sheets in the run up to the financial crisis (see, e.g., Le leslé 2012;

Liikanen et al. 2012; Noeth and Sengupta 2012; Shin 2012; European Systemic Risk Board 2014). European banks have thus reduced their dependence on loans and deposits in commercial banking, and have increasingly relied on investment banking and wholesale markets in the 2000s. Hardie and Howarth (2013) defined the changes in the balance sheets of European banks in the 2000s as a shift of commercial banking toward "market-based banking."

In terms of currency denomination, European banks expanded their balance sheets denominated largely in two currencies in the 2000s. First, they expanded their balance sheets denominated in the common currency: the euro. With respect to global banking, they expanded simultaneously both assets and liabilities on their balance sheets denominated in the euro within the Eurozone and with its neighboring countries. This development shows that currency asymmetry within the global monetary system based on the U.S. dollar standard has gradually declined, thereby facilitating the transformation of the global monetary system from the unipolar dollar standard into a multicurrency system in the long run. Correspondingly, it seems probable that the U.S. dollar standard system has been less asymmetric than it once was, at least under the Bretton Woods system (Bernanke 2015).

At the same time, it should be noted that currency asymmetry in global banking across the Atlantic was actually exacerbated in the 2000s prior to the GFC. European banks increased sharply their long-term dollar assets in the United States, whereas the demand by U.S. banks for assets denominated in European currencies has been much smaller (Baba et al. 2009). To buy long-term dollar assets, European banks came to rely heavily on short-term dollar borrowings from interbank markets, U.S. money market mutual funds (MMMFs), and foreign exchange (FX) swaps in the 2000s prior to the financial crisis (Acharya and Schnabl 2010; He and McCauley 2012; Shin 2012). Thus, European banks expanded simultaneously both assets and liabilities on their balance sheets denominated in dollars in the 2000s.

Which factors led European banks to expand their US dollar (USD)-denominated balance sheets across the Atlantic in the 2000s, despite the creation of the euro?[1] According to the view based on the hypothesis of a shortage of global safe assets (henceforth, the SGSA), there was an insufficient supply of U.S. government-guaranteed safe assets such as U.S. treasury bonds (U.S. treasuries) and U.S. agency bonds (U.S. agencies), compared to the strong demand from foreign investors, including European banks. This shortage facilitated securitization in U.S. shadow banking system endogenously to create USD-denominated debt securities that were nearly as safe as U.S. treasuries and U.S. agencies (see, e.g., Caballero 2006; Gourinchas 2010; Gordon 2015).

The SGSA view essentially suggests that the U.S. shadow banking system had the advantage endogenously to issue USD-denominated safe assets in the 2000s. However, few studies based on the SGSA view have actually analyzed what determined the currency denomination of the balance sheets of European banks. To provide such an explanation, two important issues absent from the SGCA view must be confronted. First, it is necessary to compare the U.S. shadow banking system to that of the Eurozone in the 2000s. Second, it is indispensable to examine the institutional differences in monetary policy on both sides of the Atlantic.

This article argues that the comparative advantage of U.S. shadow banking system compared to the less advanced system in the Eurozone allowed European banks to expand USD-denominated balance sheets across the Atlantic, resulting in the reign of the U.S. dollar in the shadow banking system in the 2000s. The rest of the article is structured as follows: The second section argues that the full development of securitization and wholesale funding in the United States compared to the less advanced system in the Eurozone appeared to provide European banks with opportunities for profit making within the U.S. shadow banking system, thus encouraging them to expand their USD-denominated balance sheets across the Atlantic in the 2000s and before the financial crisis. The third section shows that the evolution of the U.S. Federal Reserve system (U.S. Fed) policy reinforced the comparative advantage of the U.S. shadow banking system. The fourth section demonstrates that the unprecedented expansion of European bank balance sheets during the U.S. housing bubble in 2004–2006 allowed the banks to overstretch their USD-denominated balance sheets. The fifth section establishes the reason for the reign of the dollar in the shadow banking system in the 2000s. The last section suggests implications drawn from the arguments in the previous sections.

Comparison of the U.S. shadow banking system with the system in the Eurozone

The fuller development of the U.S. shadow banking system

Two important functions of the shadow banking system stand out compared to the traditional commercial banking system: securitization and wholesale funding (see, e.g., see Pozsar et al. 2010; Claessens et al. 2012). The U.S. shadow banking system has steadily expanded since the 1990s. Its size surpassed that of the commercial banking system after 2000 and reached more than $12 trillion in the years before the GFC of 2008 (The Financial Crisis Inquiry Commission 2011: 32). Likewise, assets of other financial intermediaries (OFIs) in the Eurozone, which are a proxy for the activities of the European shadow banking system, grew rapidly in the run up to the GFC (Bouveret 2011; Jeffers and Pilhon 2011; Bakk-Simon et al. 2012). Assets of OFIs in the Eurozone grew from €7.2 trillion in the fourth quarter of 1999 to €14.7 trillion in the fourth quarter of 2007, whereas assets of commercial banks increased from €15.0 trillion to €27.0 trillion during the same period (Deutsche Bundesbank 2014: 20). The following sections discuss whether the shadow banking system on both sides of the Atlantic could adequately fulfill its two important functions in the 2000s.

The process of securitization is conducted through off-balance sheet vehicles such as special purpose vehicles (SPVs), structured investment vehicles (SIVs), and conduits, which are used by a handful of large complex financial institutions (LCFIs) in the United States and Europe, including U.S. commercial banks, U.S. investment banks, and European banks. Securitization allows banks to turn illiquid assets into private-label debt securities, such as mortgage-backed securities (MBSs), asset-backed securities (ABSs), and collateralized debt obligations (CDOs). According to the SGSA view, there was an insufficient supply of U.S. government-guaranteed safe assets, relative to the strong demand for them by foreign investors in the 2000s. The full development of the securitization system resulted in the endogenous issuing of MBSs, ABSs, and CDOs with slightly higher returns that were almost as safe as U.S. treasuries and U.S. agencies. The global issuance of ABS reached $17.6 trillion during 1999 to 2008, more than two-thirds of which was by issuers located in the United States, and most of which were denominated in dollars (99.5%; European Central Bank 2009b: 32). Although the U.S. bond portfolio of European banks at the end of 2002 consisted mostly of U.S. treasuries and U.S. agencies, their portfolio shifted toward riskier securitized assets by mid-2007. On a nationality basis, the share of ABS in European holdings of U.S. securities reached 32 percent in June 2007, whereas the share of U.S. treasuries and U.S. agencies amounted to 26 percent (McCauley 2018: 50).

Remarkably, U.S. debt securities played a dual role on USD-denominated balance sheets. Although U.S. debt securities support a slightly higher yield on the asset side, they were also used as collateral assets to raise short-term cheaper dollar borrowings through wholesale funding on the liability side (Bayoumi and Bui 2012: 8). U.S. treasuries have played the role of "universally accepted collateral" in wholesale funding (Schinasi, Kramer, and Smith 2001: 4–5). Furthermore, U.S. agencies, all types of private-label MBSs, all types of ABSs, and tranches of structured products have also been used as collateral since the last half of the 1990s (Acharya and Öncü 2010: 330). Thus, a broad range of U.S. debt securities were used as universally accepted collateral in wholesale funding markets before the GFC.[2]

The repo market is a vital source of wholesale funding for banks and nonbanks. The use of safe assets as collateral makes borrowings in repos less costly and less risky than borrowing from unsecured money markets (Gabor and Ban 2015: 618) The repo market comprises two complementary segments: the cash-driven segment and the securities-driven segment. In the former, transactions are generally conducted against general collateral (GC)—that is, a basket of nonspecific government securities. The average spread for the three-month maturity between the interbank rate and the GC repo rate in the U.S. was 21 basis points between June 2001 and June 2002, compared to 9 basis points in the Eurozone (European Central Bank 2002: 61). The GC repo rates were also on average 5 to 10 basis points below comparable overnight index swap (OIS) rates, which provide a near risk-free benchmark for the United States prior to the mid-2007. Thus, the repo rate was close to the interbank rate, and typically slightly below it (Hördahl and King 2008: 42).

Total repo activity in the United States reached its peak before the GFC, ranging from $5 to $10 trillion (Baklanova et al. 2015: 1).

Moreover, asset-backed commercial papers (ABCPs) were an important wholesale funding source for financial institutions that relied on short-term cheaper dollar borrowing. Most European banks financed their off-balance-sheet vehicles by issuing ABCPs denominated in dollars rather than in euros. As an example, with respect to ABCPs outstanding for German banks as of January 2007, $139 billion out of $205 billion (68 percent) were denominated in dollars, whereas only $63 billion (30.7 percent) were denominated in euros (estimates from Acharya and Schnabl 2010: 55) The fuller development of securitization and wholesale funding in the U.S. shadow banking system appeared to provide European banks with opportunities for profit making in the United States.

The underdevelopment of the shadow banking system in the Eurozone

There was a shortage of safe assets denominated in euros in the Eurozone in the 2000s prior to the financial crisis. Because the issuance of government bonds in the Eurozone grew at a slower pace than the repo market, there was a rising demand for alternative, privately created debt securities as collateral assets during the period (European Central Bank 2006). Was the shadow banking system in the Eurozone capable of responding to the shortage of euro-denominated safe assets?

The introduction of the euros together with increased demand from institutional investors and financial innovation were expected to encourage the development of securitization in the Eurozone (Prati and Schinasi 1997a: 264; Altunbas, Gambacorta, and Marqués 2007: 10). New issuance of securitized assets in the European Union had increased in the 2000s, and reached at the peak in 2008 (Kozak and Teplova 2012: 35). However, securitization activity was lower in the Eurozone than in the United States before the financial crisis. Securitized issuance, for instance, amounted to €462 billion, compared with $1.7 trillion in the United States, or around 5 percent and 12 percent of GDP, respectively (Bakk-Simon et al. 2012: 13). The underdevelopment of securitization in the Eurozone was mainly due to three factors. First, European banks have retained the majority of securitized assets on their balance sheets, rather than offloading the assets to other investors. The main reason was that European banks turned illiquid assets into securitized products, and then held large part of these on-balance sheets as eligible collateral for European Central Bank (ECB) refinancing operations (European Central Bank 2011a, 2011d; Bakk-Simon et al. 2012). Second, the development of securitization in the Eurozone remained variable across countries and sectors (Altunbas, Gambacorta, and Marqués 2007: 11). Finally, institutional differences in lending criteria, banking institutions, rating standards, and default laws in the course of securitization have remained important (Hakkarainen 2014: 3). In short, the weaknesses of securitization in the Eurozone relative to the United States impeded the ability of European banks to make privately created debt securities denominated in the euro, in response to the shortage of euro-denominated safe assets in the Eurozone in the 2000s. Between 1999 and 2008, the issuance of ABSs in the Eurozone amounted to no more than $1,867 billion, in contrast to $11,983 billion in the United States (European Central Bank 2009b: 32).

Institutional developments in wholesale funding were expected to spur growth of the Eurozone-wide repo market in the 2000s. Even though the introduction of the euro induced expansion of wholesale financial markets, encouraging the unsecured money market and government bond markets to be closely integrated, there remained several areas that were insufficiently integrated (Schinasi and Teixeira 2006: 3). As (Gabor and Ban 2015: 623) suggested, "[I]n an area characterized by a single currency, old rules and market architectures may be unsuited to the task and become instead the main obstacles to the attainment of a higher degree of efficiency."

According to The Giovannini Group (1999: 1), "The repo market is a perfect illustration of this problem." To support establishment of a Eurozone-wide repo market, the Eurozone initiated a series of institutional reforms through "a private–public joint venture" prior to the GFC (Gabor 2016a). Specifically, the European Commission launched the Financial Services Action Plan (FSAP) in 1999, which was a set of legislative-regulatory harmonization policies aimed at tackling the last remaining obstacles to the integration of the wholesale market. Above all, the FSAP's legislative agenda included the planned adoption of new directives on the cross-border use of collateral and market manipulation (European Central Bank

2012: 37). Additionally, the ECB from the outset accepted a broader range of collateral in its open market operations than other central banks in advanced countries, thus promoting the development of Eurozone-wide repo markets (Eichengreen 1997: 18; Prati and Schinasi 1997a: 276; Gabor 2016b: 931–932). In this connection, the ECB created a euro general collateral basket called by "Euro GC Polling" that included all Economic and Monetary Union government bonds in the same liquidity category, encouraging private repo market activity. This development facilitated repo transactions via a central counterparty (CCP) and offered an automated cross-border collateral management system allowing banks to reuse GC collateral as well as pledging collateral with the ECB (Hördahl and King 2008: 48). Repo participants increasingly used foreign government bonds in the Eurozone as collateral. The share of cross-border euro repos increased their share from 36 percent in 2001 to 48 percent in 2008, whereas "home" collateral declined from 63 percent to 31 percent during the period (Gabor and Ban 2015: 625). Hence, the outstanding volume in the European repo market (repo plus reverse repo positions) increased from €1,863 billion in June 2001 to €6,775 billion in June 2007 (data from International Capital Market Association European Repo Market Survey website).

Nevertheless, similarly to the underdevelopment of securitization, significant barriers and constraints to the development of Eurozone-wide repo market remained in the 2000s. First, although the ECB accepted a broader range of collateral through its open market operations, most collateral in private repo markets in the Eurozone consisted of government bonds. According to average collateral usage during 2006 in primary and secondary funding, ECB collateral consisted of central government bonds, regional government bonds, uncovered and covered bank bonds, corporate bonds, ABS, and so on. By contrast, collateral asset usage of privately produced debt securities in the private repo market in European Union reached only 15.8 percent, whereas central government bonds accounted for 84.2 percent in 2006 (Ewehart and Tapking 2008: 54).

Second, the ECB became more selective about government bonds in the Eurozone used as eligible collateral in its refinancing operations after December 2005. The ECB stipulated that government bonds must have a single A-rating, or better, from at least one of three rating agencies (*Financial Times*, November 9, 2005), as Cohen (2011) suggested.

Finally, many barriers to efficient cross-border securities settlement remained unaddressed, which meant that Europe could not establish an integrated wholesale funding market (European Central Bank 2014; International Capital Market Association 2014).

Insufficient integration and fragmented infrastructure for European securities settlement resulted in higher cost of clearing and settlement across borders in the European Union compared to United States and domestic EU clearing and settlement. Cross-border costs in the European Union range from €19.5 to €35.0, whereas domestic EU costs range from €0.35 to €3.43, and U.S. costs amount from €0.10 to €2.90 (European Central Bank 2007: 6). It is likely that the underdevelopment of private repo market in the Eurozone did not allow European banks to finance their operations at interest rates below those in unsecured interbank markets. In short, the underdevelopment of securitization and wholesale funding within the shadow banking system of the Eurozone reduced profit-making opportunities for European banks.

It follows from the comparative analysis of shadow banking on both sides of the Atlantic that the fuller development of securitization and wholesale funding in the United States provided European banks with the opportunities for profit making in the U.S. shadow banking system. The comparative advantage of the U.S. shadow banking system compared to the less advanced system of the Eurozone encouraged European banks to expand their USD-denominated balance sheets across the Atlantic in the 2000s prior to the financial crisis.

The evolution of U.S. Fed policy encouraging the development of the shadow banking system

The function of lender of last resort in the development of the shadow banking system

The U.S. shadow banking system has expanded greatly since the 1990s. The development of the shadow banking system contributed to shadow financial intermediation becoming longer lasting and more variegated in the United States compared to the traditional commercial banking system. Thus, the interconnectedness between various financial institutions, particularly the nexus between banks and nonbanks, rose commensurately (see Adrian and Shin 2010: 1–5; Claessens et al. 2012: 8) The increase in the interconnectedness within the shadow banking system resulted in the buildup of systemic risk, arising from bank failure and default, which has led to the recurrence of financial crisis.

The recurrence of crises has raised the need for a central bank to counter financial distress. Commercial banks were able to access the central bank's refinancing facilities and deposit insurance in time of financial crisis, but nonbanks within the U.S. shadow banking system were not able to access this liquidity backstop. Along with the development of shadow banking system, it became necessary for the central bank to assume the function of lender of last resort (LLR) in the course of countercyclical monetary policy, with the aim of rescuing not only commercial banks but also nonbanks faced with systemic risk. The function of the LLR, which was recognized by Walter Bagehot in the 19th century, refers to the central bank's responsibility to accommodate credit demands for high-powered money from banks in time of crisis (Humphrey 1992). The Fed has expanded the scope of the LLR to support the development of the U.S. shadow banking system since the 1990s. Along similar lines, it was necessary for the European Central Bank (ECB) to play the role of the LLR in the Eurozone in view of the rapid evolution of EMU in the 1990s, which relied on European financial markets becoming more liquid and securitization developing further (Folkerts-Landau and Garber 1992: 31). In short, it became crucial for both the Fed and the ECB to play the role of the LLR as the shadow banking system developed on both sides of the Atlantic. But their respective roles unfolded quite differently in the 2000s.

The U.S. Fed understands fully that the function of the LLR goes beyond the scope of stabilizing U.S. commercial banks (Folkerts-Landau and Garber 1992: 25). Furthermore, the Fed comprehends implicitly that it has the responsibility of playing the role of "international lender of last resort" for non-U.S. banks.[3] According to Broz (2012: 8),

> [T]he Federal Reserve Act of 1913 gave the Federal Reserve responsibility for both setting monetary policy and for maintaining the stability of financial markets. In the latter, the Fed supervises U.S. and non-U.S. banks and bank holding companies that are members of the Federal Reserve System and provides a role of the LLR to these institutions during financial crises.

Since the Mexico currency crisis of 1982, the U.S. Fed has played the role of the international LLR. (Strange 1986/2016: 151; Papaioannou and Portes 2008: 71–73; Obstfelt 2009: 12–13). At the time of the subprime mortgage crisis in the summer of 2007 and the GFC of 2008, the Fed provided a massive amount of LLR loans to foreign financial institutions, especially European banks, which were experiencing severe dollar funding shortages (Broz 2012: 7–8). Thus, the function of LLR delivered by the U.S. Fed was able to backstop not only for U.S. financial institutions but also for non-U.S. financial institutions faced with financial failure.

Consider now the impact of the institutional framework of the Eurosystem on the ability of the ECB to act fully as LLR in the Eurozone. The Maastricht Treaty signed in February 1992, which was the blueprint for advancing toward EMU, provided the legal basis for the European System of Central Banks (ESCB), which comprises the ECB and the national central banks (NCBs) of member states of the EU. The "Eurosystem" stands for a subset of the ESCB that comprises the ECB and the NCBs of countries that have adopted the euro (Gerdesmeier, Francesco Paolo, and Barbara 2007: 8). The basic tasks of the Eurosystem include implementation of monetary policy, conducting foreign exchange operations, holding and managing the official foreign reserves, and promoting the smooth operation of payment systems (Article 105.2. of the Maastricht Treaty).

Although the institutional framework of the Eurosystem appears to be similar to other central banks in advanced countries, monetary policy in the Eurosystem is decentralized. One of the features of decentralization in the Eurosystem lies in the segmented framework in monetary policy. Although monetary policy is entrusted to the ECB, the responsibility for banking supervision is still kept in the hands of the NCBs (Moutot, Jung, and Mongelli 2008: 18–19). This decentralized structure in monetary policy raises the concern that the ECB could not play sufficiently the function of the LLR in times of crisis. Instead, the Eurosystem provided emergency liquidity assistance (ELA), which was summed up as follows by the European Central Bank (1999: 98):

> Co-ordination mechanisms are primarily called for within the Eurosystem. This is the case for emergency liquidity assistance (ELA), which embraces the support given by central banks in exceptional circumstances and on a case-by-case basis to temporarily illiquid institutions and markets. At the outset, it is necessary to stress that the importance of ELA should not be overemphasized. … The main guiding principle is that the competent NCB takes the decision concerning the provision of ELA to an institution operating in its jurisdiction. This would take place under the responsibility and at the cost of the NCB in question.

It follows that, although the advance of ELA could be considered as exceptional provision of central bank liquidity to a solvent bank facing temporary liquidity problems, it is far from clear that the ECB could advance ELA in face of financial crisis. This unclear stance of the central bank regarding the provision of liquidity is called "constructive ambiguity." The stance is based on the concern that overly generous LLR assistance might generate moral hazard among financial institutions, allowing them to encourage excessive leverage and risk taking (IMF 2014: 102). In order to avoid moral hazard, policymakers introduced ambiguity in the implementation of the LLR.

Could the ECB play the role of the LLR in face of Eurozone-wide financial crisis? On the one hand, Papadoa-Schioppa (2000) stressed that Articles 105.5 and 105.6 of the Maastricht Treaty seem to ensure that "the competent authorities" pursue a smooth interplay between monetary policy and supervisory responsibilities. If these articles were followed fully, the concern about the separation of monetary policy from banking supervisory responsibilities would disappear. Hence, the procedure defined by the Maastricht Treaty could be interpreted as a "last resort clause," which enables the ECB to play the role of the LLR. (Papadoa-Schioppa 2000: 17–18) On the other hand, Aglietta (2000) insisted that the Maastricht Treaty gives the ECB only a limited role to counter Eurozone-wide systemic risk. Although the possible contribution of the ECB to financial stability is mentioned in Articles 105.5 and 105.6, policies toward this purpose supposed to be implemented by "competent authorities" were not defined. Thus, the LLR function was not clearly identified in the Eurosystem. (Aglietta 2000: 47)

So, could the ECB play the role of the LLR? As noted, responsibility for ELA lies with the NCBs, not the ECB. Any costs and risks arising from ELA operations are incurred by the NCBs themselves.[4] Due to this flaw in the provision of ELA, the ECB was forced to operate its monetary policy by cutting short-term interest rates and deploying its regular refinancing operations, rather than ELA, as it sought to support commercial banks in the course of the subprime mortgage crisis in 2007 and until the GFC of 2008 (Herr 2013: 70). The articles of the Maastricht Treaty and the mechanism of ELA proved dysfunctional in countering the GFC, thus causing serious damage to European banks. It seems imperative for the Eurosystem to create a mechanism that could tackle Eurozone-wide crises. Based on this analysis, the ambiguity of the ECB's stance regarding the function of the LLR could be considered as destructive rather than constructive.[5]

It is clear that the U.S. Fed can be expected to intervene forcefully to rescue large complex financial institutions, including European banks, when they face trouble related to the U.S. shadow banking system. In contrast, the ECB has a major institutional flaw in delivering the role of LLR fully, although it is able to make decisions on ELA.

The 'too-big-to-fail' policy

In essence, the LLR policy rule is that the central bank should lend freely at penalty rates against good collateral in order to save solvent but temporarily illiquid banks. But the U.S. Fed has increasingly lent to insolvent large banks of doubtful soundness, particularly when such large banks were judged as "too big to fail." The U.S. Fed and the U.S. government have adopted the doctrine of too big to fail (TBTF) since the 1980s, which goes far beyond the function of the LLR. Paul Volker, probably the most powerful chairman of the Fed during the last several decades, introduced the TBTF policy in the face of Mexico crisis and the bankruptcy of Continental Illinois at the beginning of the 1980s (Mallaby 2016: 301).

The TBTF policy is based on the belief that the failure of large banks has a negative impact on the financial system. The central bank and the government should do whatever it takes to prevent this negative impact, even if a financial bailout must be paid by the taxpayers. Although the TBTF policy could indeed rescue the financial system, it is inevitable that the

TBTF policy would give Wall Street financial institutions and large European banks implicit protection of their USD-denominated assets by U.S. policymakers in the face of financial distress (Obstfelt 2009: 11). Large European banks and U.S. banks enjoyed higher *ex-ante* safety-net benefits through the TBTF policy in 2003–2008 (Carbo-Valverde, Kane, and Rodriguez-Fernandez 2011). The *de facto* insurance offered through the TBTF policy could allow banks to obtain cheaper funding—thus increasing leverage on the liability side—and to engage in riskier activities on the asset side (IMF 2014: 103–104). It seems safe to infer that the TBTF policy offers to European banks the implicit certainty that their dollar assets in the U.S. shadow banking system would be supported by U.S. policymakers in the face of financial crisis.

The 'Greenspan put'

In addition, the Fed under the leadership of Alan Greenspan executed a peculiar monetary policy in the 2000s. The Fed cut short-term federal funds (FF) rates aggressively after the collapse of the Long-Term Capital Management hedge fund in 1998 and the burst of the technology bubble in 2000, aiming to prevent deflation. Immediately after the burst of the technology bubble, the Fed cut the FF rate by 50 basis points in early January 2001, and then eased intermittently, bringing it down to .98 percent in December 2003 (data from Federal Reserve Bank of St. Louis, Economic Research website). This is an example of what came to be known as the "Greenspan put"—namely, that the Fed would cut the FF rates sharply after the burst of a bubble.[6]

O'Driscoll (2009) and Buttonwood (2017) noted that the Greenspan put can be regarded as "the asymmetric" monetary policy (O'Driscoll 2009: 179). The Fed would not stop the asset bubble because it professes not to know when financial markets are in bubble territory. In contrast, the Fed is certain to cut the FF rate drastically to prevent deflation when the markets had fallen too far. Greenspan (2002: 8–9) stated the following:

> [T]he Federal Reserve has focused on policies that would, as I testified before the Congress in 1999, "… mitigate the fallout [of an asset bubble] when it occurs and, hopefully, ease the transition to the next expansion." The Federal Open Market Committee chose, as you know, to embark on an aggressive course of monetary easing two years ago once it became apparent that a variety of forces, including importantly the slump in household wealth that resulted from the decline in stock prices, were restraining inflation pressures and economic activity.

Wall Street financial institutions welcomed the Greenspan put "because it meant that he would not raise interest rates preemptively to choke off a boom" (Johnson and Kwak 2010: 101–102). It was likely that the

Greenspan put would trigger a new asset bubble, thus reviving financial profits of Wall Street financial institutions and European banks.

Summing up, the LLR and the TBTF strategy gave European banks implicit assurance that their USD-denominated assets would be protected by U.S. policymakers in the face of financial distress. Meanwhile, the Greenspan put would trigger the next asset bubble, thus reviving financial profits. To put it differently, the evolution of the U.S. Fed policy reinforced the comparative advantage of the U.S. shadow banking system compared to the less developed shadow banking system of the Eurozone.

The self-expansion mechanism of USD-denominated balance sheets in the course of the U.S. housing bubble

The comparative advantage of the U.S. shadow banking system relative to the less advanced Eurozone shadow banking system led European banks to stretch their USD-denominated balance sheets across the Atlantic. The U.S. housing bubble from 2004 to 2006, marked by a swift upsurge in housing prices, accelerated the overstretch of the USD-denominated balance sheets of European banks. U.S. debt securities played a dual role: They supported a slightly high yield on the asset side, but they also functioned as collateral for cheaper short-term dollar borrowing on the liability side. The rapid increase in the prices of U.S. debt securities used as collateral—driven by the U.S. housing bubble—created excess capacity among large complex financial institutions, in the sense that their equity became larger than the amount required to meet their value-at-risk (VAR) constraint. In response to this excess capacity, large complex financial institutions actively adjusted their balance sheets by increasing the overall size, rather than paying out the surplus equity in the form of higher dividends (Adrian and Shin 2010: 17–18; Shin 2010: 119–120). Large complex financial institutions, including European banks, reached an unprecedented capacity during the housing bubble in the U.S. shadow banking system.

What was the response of European banks to the unprecedented capacity of their USD-denominated balance sheets? They appear to have pursued excessive leverage, thus boosting the return on equity (ROE), given the slight margin in balance sheets. In fact, the precise margins of European banks were estimated at only between 10 and 30 basis points (Thiemann 2012: 44). On the assets side, the off-balance-sheet vehicles created by European banks sought to purchase private-label U.S. debt securities, which appeared to be nearly as safe as U.S. treasuries and U.S. agencies. Thus, Wall Street financial institutions could create further MBSs, ABSs, and CDOs, largely through the origination and securitization of risky and long-term subprime mortgages in the U.S. shadow banking system. As a result, the gross issuance of global private-label securitization reached a peak of nearly $5 trillion in 2006 (IMF 2011: 13).

Two mechanisms sustained private-label securitization based on subprime mortgages. First, high credit ratings allowed large complex financial institutions to successfully sell U.S. debt securities, which were securitized from subprime mortgages, to other investors (White 2009). Second, large complex financial institutions bought large amounts of credit default swaps (CDSs) on ABSs and CDOs, written by insurance companies such as American International Group (AIG). Thus, they hedged the credit risk associated with the underlying assets: the subprime mortgages. The main counterparties of AIG were large complex financial institutions in the United States and Europe, including Société Générale, Deutsche Bank, Goldman Sachs, Merrill Lynch, Calyon, Barclays, and UBS (IMF 2011: 9).

Consequently, on the liability side, the U.S. housing bubble accelerated further and led to rising market values and the erosion of haircuts/margins of U.S. debt securities functioning as collateral, thus enabling European banks to raise cheaper short-term dollar borrowing. In June 2007, immediately prior to the subprime mortgage crisis, the erosion of haircuts/margins of the prime MBSs, ABSs, structured assets (AAA), and investment grade bonds was reported from 1 to 10 percent (The Committee on the Global Financial System 2010: 2). Intensive growth of collateral intermediation at the central desk of large complex financial institutions supported the "mining" of collateral assets and the reuse of collateral (i.e., rehypothecation), thus allowing European banks to raise ever larger amounts of cheap short-term dollar borrowings (Singh 2011; European Commission 2013). The rehypothecation of collateral generated a rapid rise in intrafinancial sector transactions, driving European banks to pursue excessive leverage. The level of leverage at European large complex financial institutions reached more than 45 times equity at its peak in the 2000s, whereas the level of leverage at U.S. securities house and U.S. commercial banks amounted to more than 30 times and 15 times, respectively, in the 2000s (Haldane 2010, Chart 24).

Based on these developments, a self-expansion mechanism emerged for European bank USD-denominated balance sheets during the U.S. housing bubble.[7] A stylized example of the self-expansion mechanism in USD-denominated balance sheets is illustrated in Figure 1.

In short, long-term U.S. private-label debt securities, created through securitization, played a dual role in the USD-denominated balance sheets of European banks. U.S. debt securities were used as collateral assets to raise short-term cheaper dollar borrowing. The SIVs of European banks subsequently used the dollars to invest again in long-term U.S. private-label debt securities. The U.S. housing bubble encouraged European banks to

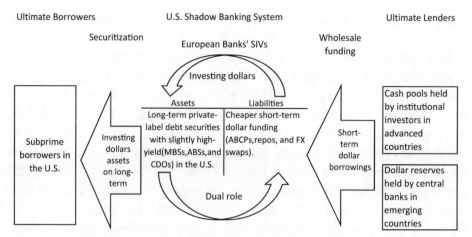

Figure 1. A Stylized Example of the Self-Expansion Mechanism of European Banks' USD-denominated Balance Sheets during the U.S. Housing Bubble.

amplify the self-expansion of their USD-denominated balance sheets, as the housing bubble drove higher the prices of debt securities in the U.S. shadow banking system. The self-expansion mechanism led European banks to overstretch their USD-denominated balance sheets, thus reaping the opportunities for profit making in the U.S. shadow banking system. The level of ROE at large complex financial institutions in the U.S. and Europe was consistently at or above 20%, which was roughly double the ROE in the nonfinancial sector (Haldane 2010, 13). Thus, the overstretching of USD-denominated balance sheets allowed European banks to achieve a higher ROE.

The reign of the U.S. dollar in the shadow banking system in the 2000s

The overstretching of USD-denominated balance sheets in the course of the U.S. housing bubble sustained the strong demand for long-term private-label debt securities and short-term financial instruments denominated in U.S. dollars.[8] Several factors led to this development.

First, USD-denominated long-term ABS issuances increased in unprecedented fashion. The share of the dollar in ABS issuance rose from around 65 percent in 1999 to 75 to 80 percent on the eve of the financial crisis, while the share of the euro increased gradually from around 15 percent to about 20 percent during the same period (European Central Bank 2011c: 52, Chart 25).

Second, USD-denominated short-term financial instruments, such as ABCPs, grew rapidly in the 2000s and prior to the GFC. In total, with respect to ABCPs outstanding by funding currency as of January 2007,

$714 billion out of $969 billion (or 73.7 percent) were denominated in dollars, and only $219 billion (or 22.6 percent) in euros (estimates from Acharya and Schnabl 2010: 55, Table 4).

Third, the dollar played the dominant role as collateral asset in the global repo market in the 2000s. Judging by the liabilities and the equity of, respectively, the U.S. domestic economy and the rest of the world in June 2007, foreign holdings of treasury bonds were the largest proportion of the amount outstanding (45 percent). The share of agency bonds, corporate bonds (nonasset-backed), and corporate ABS + ABCP reached 21 percent, 25 percent, and 22 percent, respectively (Beltran, Pounder, and Thomas 2008: 24, Table 3). Taking into account the higher share of foreigners in the holdings of U.S. debt securities, a broad range of U.S. debt securities was used as universally accepted collateral in the global repo market in the 2000s and prior to the GFC.

Finally, the dominant position of the dollar in the foreign exchange (FX) swaps market allowed European banks to borrow massively in dollars. When non-U.S. banks raise U.S. dollar borrowings through secured transactions, they often use FX swaps to exchange domestic currency for dollars. As an example, European banks would buy dollars by selling euros for dollars in the spot exchange market, and then sell dollars to buy back euros in the forward exchange market. These transactions can be considered as collateralized short-term dollar borrowing, due to the funding of dollar acquisitions by providing domestic currency—that is, euros (Ando 2012). Judging by the use of U.S. dollars and euros in European foreign exchange markets in April 2007, several European currencies—such as the Danish krone, the Norwegian krone, the Polish zloty, and the Swedish krona—traded more heavily in euros than dollars in the spot market. In contrast, FX swap markets in Europe traded more heavily in dollars (McCauley 2012, 99). Thus, European banks tended to rely on FX swaps to obtain dollars against euros and other European currencies.

In all, the strong demand for long-term private-label U.S. debt securities (MBSs, ABSs, and CDOs) and short-term U.S. financial instruments (repos, ABCPs, and FX swaps) contributed to the reign of the U.S. dollar in the shadow banking system. It seems natural to conclude that the U.S. dollar standard system remained as asymmetric as ever in the 2000s, contrary to the view that the asymmetry abated, as Bernanke (2015) claimed.

Implications

Several implications follow from the preceding analysis. First, through the expansion of their USD-denominated balance sheets, European banks played the role of USD-denominated global financial intermediary in the 2000s, as U.S. banks had done in the 1960s (Kindleberger, Despres, and

Salant 1966). It is well known that U.K. banks from the middle of the 19th to the beginning of the 20th century, and U.S. banks after the end of World War II, played the role of global financial intermediaries, their activities denominated mostly in their own currencies: the pound sterling and the U.S. dollar, respectively (Tavlas and Ozeki 1992). During the 2000s, European banks played the role of financial intermediary across the Atlantic, but their activities were denominated in a foreign currency—that is, the dollar and not the euro.[9] European banks relent the dollars across the Atlantic, playing a role similar to that of the Japanese banks that had acted as USD-denominated global financial intermediaries in the second half of the 1980s (Nakao 1991/1995).

Second, the "exorbitant privilege" of the United States reflected in the dominant position of the dollar in the shadow banking system was directed toward meeting credit demands associated with the U.S. housing bubble. The dominant position of the dollar in the shadow banking system facilitated massive private capital inflows from Europe to the United States in the courses of the U.S. housing bubble (2004–2006). Private capital inflows from Europe to the United States surged from $644 billion in 2001–2003 to $1,503 billion in 2004–2006, rising from 43.6 percent to 50.0 percent in total U.S. private capital inflows (estimates from U.S. Bureau of Economic Analysis website).

The government of George W. Bush claimed that capital inflows in the United States could be used to support higher domestic investment. According to Council of Economic Advisors (2004: 260), "[T]he availability of foreign investment permitted the United States to maintain higher investment rates than it could have funded relying solely on domestic financing. These capital inflows have helped finance U.S. investments, expand U.S. productive capacity, and strengthen U.S. economic performance." In practice, private capital inflows in the course of the U.S. housing bubble not only allowed the U.S. household sector to accumulate debts beyond their means but also allowed Wall Street financial institutions and European banks to overstretch their USD-denominated balance sheets, thus achieving higher profits in the 2000s. The largest recipient of foreign credit immediately prior to the financial crisis was the U.S. financial sector. In 2007, roughly 60 percent of U.S. private-label debt securities outstanding were owned by the U.S. financial sector (Bhatia and Bayoumi 2012: 15, 23). The bulk of capital inflows from Europe, underpinned by the reign of the dollar in the shadow banking system, were used by the U.S. financial sector in relation to the housing bubble rather than to promote productive investment in the U.S. economy.

Notes

1. Maes (2015) pointed out that the expansion of USD-denominated balance sheets at European banks in the 2000s seems to outpace any reasonable growth based on standard views about the choice of international currency.

2. In addition to U.S. debt securities, collateral was widened to include foreign paper when the Basel Committee loosened its capital requirements for repos in July 2005. This regulatory change enabled foreign banks to participate in U.S. repo market (Bayoumi 2017/2018: 75)

3. Kindleberger (1978/2005) described the long history of the international lender of last resort.

4. The former presidents of the ECB, Duisenberg and Trichet, stressed that the ECB will not act as a role of the LLR (see Pollard 2003: 19; Barber and Atkins 2011)

5. De Grauwe (2013) insisted that the ECB should play a role of the lender of last resort in government bond markets of the monetary union.

6. The Greenspan put is based on the experience of deflation in Japan in the 1990s. (Greenspan 2007)

7. The mechanism was also explored in detail by Adrian and Shin (2010), the Committee on the Global Financial System (2011), Cömert (2013), and the European Systemic Risk Board (2014).

8. Most of the material in this section draws on Tokunaga and Epstein (2018).

9. Cohen (2011) suggested that the multicurrency system in the 2000s, consisting of the dollar and the euro, can be regarded as "a one-and-a-half" global monetary system.

Acknowledgments

I would like to thank Gerald Epstein and Takuyoshi Takada for helpful and constructive comments on an earlier draft. The core argument of this article was presented at the Union of Radical Political Economy (URPE) 50th Anniversary Conference & Celebration on September 2018 at the University of Massachusetts, Amherst. I am grateful for the useful comments by participants. I would also like to thank two referees and the editor for helpful comments. All remaining errors are my responsibility.

References

Acharya, V. V., and T. S. Öncü. 2010. "The Repurchase Agreement (Repo Market)." In *Regulating Wall Street: The Dodd-Frank Act and the New Architecture of Global Finance*, edited by V. V. Acharya, T. F. Cooley, M. P. Richardson, and I. Walter. Hoboken, NJ: John Wiley and Sons, pp. 319–50.

Acharya, V. V., and P. Schnabl. 2010. "Do Global Banks Spread Global Imbalances? Asset Backed Commercial Paper during the Financial Crisis of 2007–2009." *IMF Economic Review* 58 (1):37–73. doi: 10.1057/imfer.2010.4.

Adrian, T., and H. S. Shin. 2010. "The Changing Nature of Financial Intermediation and the Financial Crisis of 2007-09," *Federal Reserve Bank of New York Staff Reports*, No. 439, March 2010. pp. 1–39.

Aglietta, M. 2000. "A Lender of Last Resort for Europe." In *Which Lender of Last Resort for Europe?*, edited by C.A.E. Goodhart. London: Central Banking Publication, pp. 33–67.

Altunbas, Y., L. Gambacorta, and D. Marqués. 2007. "Securitisation and the Bank Lending Channel," *ECB Working Paper Series*, No. 383, December 2007.

Ando, M. 2012. "Recent Developments in U.S. Dollar Funding Costs through FX Swaps," *Bank of Japan Review*, 2012-E-3, April 2012.

Arteta, C., M. Carey, R. Correa, and J. Kotter. 2013. "Revenge of the Steamroller ABCP as a Window on Risk Choices." International Finance Discussion Papers Board of Governors of the Federal Reserve System. No. 1076, April 2013.

Baba, N., R. N. McCauley, and S. Ramaswamy. 2009. "US Dollar Money Market Funds and non-US Banks." BIS Quarterly Review 65–80.

Bakk-Simon, K., S. Borgioli, C. Giron, H. Hempell, A. Maddaloni, F. Recine, and S. Rosati. 2012. "Shadow Banking System in the Euro Area: An Overview." Occasional Paper Series European Central Bank, No. 133, April 2012.

Baklanova, V., A. Copeland, and R. McCaughrin. 2015. "Reference Guide to U.S. Repo and Securities Lending Markets," Federal Reserve Bank of New York Staff Report, No. 740, September 2015.

Barber, L., and R. Atkins. 2011. "FT Interview: Jean-Claude Trichet," Financial Times, October 13, 2011.

Bayoumi, T. 2017/2018. Unfinished Business. New Haven, CT: Yale University Press.

Bayoumi, T., and T. Bui. 2012. "Apocalypse Then: The Evolution of the North Atlantic Economy and the Global Crisis," IMF Working Paper, 11/212, September 2011.

Beltran, D. O., L. Pounder, and C. Thomas. 2008. "Foreign Exposure to Asset-Backed Securities of U.S. Origin," International Finance Discussion Paper, Board of Governors of the Federal Reserve System, No. 939, August 2008.

Bernanke, B. S. 2015. Federal Reserve Policy in an International Context, Paper presented at the 16th Jacques Polak Annual Research Conference Hosted by the International Monetary Fund, Washington DC, November 5–6, 2015.

Bertaut, C., L. P. DeMarco, S. Kamin, and R. Tryon. 2011. "ABS Inflows to the United States and the Global Financial Crisis," International Finance Discussion Papers, Board of Governors of the Federal Reserve System, No. 1028, August 2011.

Bhatia, A. V., and T. Bayoumi. 2012. "Leverage What Leverage: A Deep Dive into the U.S. Flow of Funds in Search of Clues to the Global Crisis," IMF Working Paper, 12/162, June 2012.

Bouveret, A. 2011. An Assessment of the Shadow Banking Sector in Europe, July 2011.

Broz, J. L. 2012. The Federal Reserve as Global Lender of Last Resort, the conference on "Governing the Federal Reserve," October 4–5, 2012, Nuffield College, Oxford University.

Buttonwood, 2017. "The Greenspan Legacy: The Fed Chairman's Record is a Case Study in Cognitive Dissonance," The Economist, January 5 2017.

Caballero, R. J. 2006. "On the Macroeconomics of Asset Shortages," NBER Working Paper Series, No.12753, December 2006.

Carbo-Valverde, S., E. J. Kane, and F. Rodriguez-Fernandez. 2011. "Safety-net Benefits Conferred on Difficult-to-fail-and-unwind Banks in the US and EU before and during the Great Recession," NBER Working Paper, No. 16787, February 2011.

Claessens, S., Z. Pozsar, L. Ratnovski, and M. Singh. 2012. "Shadow Banking: Economics and Policy," Staff Discussion Note, IMF, December 2012.

Cohen, B. J. 2011. The Future of Global Currency: The Euro versus the Dollar. New York, NY: Routledge.

Council of Economic Advisors. 2004. Economic Report of the President: Transmitted to the Congress. Washington DC: U.S. Government Printing Office.

Cömert, H. 2013. Central Banks and Financial Markets: The Declining Power of US Monetary Policy. Cheltenham, UK/Northampton, MA: Edward Elgar.

De Grauwe, P. 2013. "The European Central Bank as Lender of Last Resort in the Government Bond Markets." CESifo Economic Studies 59 (3):520–35. doi: 10.1093/cesifo/ift012.

Deutsche Bundesbank. 2014. "The Shadow Banking System in the Euro Area: Overview and Monetary Policy Implications", *Deutsche Bundesbank Monthly Report*, March 2014, pp. 15–34.

Eichengreen, B. 1997. The Euro as a Reserve Currency, November, 1997.

European Central Bank. 1999. Annual Report.

European Central Bank. 2002. "Main Features of the Repo Market in the Euro Area," *Monthly Bulletin*, ECB, October 2002, pp. 55–68.

European Central Bank. 2006. "Box 7: The Widening of the Collateral Pool for Secured Lending in the Euro Area." Financial Stability Review 71–73.

European Central Bank. 2007. TARGET 2 Securities Blueprint, 8 March 2007.

European Central Bank. 2009b. "The International Role of the Euro in the Market for Asset-Backed Securities." *The International Role of the Euro* 31–34.

European Central Bank. 2011a. Recent Developments Securitisation, February 2011.

European Central Bank. 2011c. The International Role of the Euro, July 2011.

European Central Bank. 2011d. "The Supply of Money–Bank Behaviour and the Implications for Monetary Analysis." *Monthly Bulletin ECB* 63–79.

European Central Bank. 2012. Financial Integration in Europe, April 2012.

European Central Bank. 2014. Euro Repo Market Improvements for Collateral and Liquidity Management, July 2014.

European Commission. 2013. Shadow Banking – Addressing New Sources of Risk in the Financial Sector, Brussels, 4.9.2013 COM (2013) 614 final.

European Systemic Risk Board. 2013. "European Banks Use of US Dollar Funding Systemic Risk Issues." Macro-Prudential Commentaries No.5, March 2013.

European Systemic Risk Board. 2014. "Is Europe Overbanked?" *Reports of the Advisory Scientific Committee*, No.4, June 2014.

Ewehart, C., and J. Tapking. 2008. "Repo Markets, Counterparty Risk and the 2007/2008 Liquidity Crisis," *ECB Working Paper Series*, No.909, June 2008.

Folkerts-Landau, D., and P. M. Garber. 1992. "The European Central Bank or a Monetary Policy Rule," *NBER Working Papers Series*, No.4016, March 1992.

Gabor, D. 2016. "A Step Too Far: The European Financial Transactions Tax on Shadow Banking." *Journal of European Public Policy* 23 (6):925–45. doi: 10.1080/13501763.2015.1070894.

Gabor, D. 2016. "The (Impossible) Repo Trinity: The Political Economy of Repo Markets." *Review of International Political Economy* 23 (6):967–1000. doi: 10.1080/09692290.2016.1207699.

Gabor, D., and C. Ban. 2015. " "Banking on Bonds: The New Links between States and Markets." *Journal of Common Market Studies* 53(4): 617–635. doi:10.1111/jcms.12309

Gerdesmeier, D., M. Francesco Paolo, and R. Barbara. 2007. "The Eurosystem, the US Federal Reserve and the Bank of Japan: Similarities and Differences," *Working paper series*, ECB, No. 742, March 2007.

Gordon, G. 2015. Mobile Collateral versus Immobile Collateral, June 2015 BIS Annual Conference in Lucerne, Switzerland, April 27, 2015.

Gourinchas, P.-O. 2010. "U.S. Monetary Policy, 'Imbalance' and the Financial Crisis," Remarks Prepared for the Financial Crisis Inquiry Commission Forum, February 26–27, 2010.

Greenspan, A. 2002. Remarks by Chairman Alan Greenspan, before the Economic Club of New York, New York City, December 19, 2002, pp. 1–16.

Greenspan, A. 2007. *The Age of Turbulence*. New York, NY: The Penguin Press.

Hakkarainen, P. 2014. Shadow Banking – what kind of Regulation for the (European) Shadow Banking System? BIS Central Bankers' Speeches, the Panel Discussion at the SAFE Summer Academy 2014 "Shadow Banking: Evolution, Background, Perspectives," Brussels, 3 September 2014.

Haldane, A. 2010. "The Contribution of the Financial Sector Miracle or Mirage?" at the Future of Finance Conference, London, 14 July 2010.

Hardie, I., and D. Howarth. 2013. "Framing Market-Based Banking and the Financial Crisis." In *Market-Based Banking and the International Financial Crisis*, edited by I. Hardie and D. Howwarth. Oxford, UK: Oxford University Press, pp. 22–55.

He, D., and R. N. McCauley. 2012. "Eurodollar Banking and Currency internationalization." BIS Quarterly Review 2012:33–46.

Herr, H. 2013. "The European Central Bank and the US Federal Reserve as Lender of Last Resort." *Panoeconomicus* 2014 (1):59–78. doi: 10.2298/PAN1401059H.

Hördahl, P., and M. R. King. 2008. "Developments in Repo Markets during the Financial Turmoil." *BIS Quarterly Review* 2008:37–53.

Humphrey, T. M. 1992. "Lender of Last Resort." In *The New Palgrave Dictionary of Money and Finance*, edited by P. K. Newman, M. Milgate and J. Eatwell, Vol. 2. London, NY: Macmillan, Stockton Press, pp. 571–3.

IMF. 2011. The Multilateral Aspects of Policies Affecting Capital Flows—Background Paper, 21 October 2011.

IMF. 2014. Global Financial Stability Report, October 2014.

International Capital Market Association. 2014. "Collateral is the New Cash: The Systemic Risks of Inhibiting Collateral Fluidity," April 2014, pp. 1–27.

Jeffers, E., and D. Plihon. 2011. What is so Special about European Shadow Banking? https://www.aeaweb.org/conference/2016/retrieve.php?pdfid=1294

Johnson, S., and J. Kwak. 2010. *13 Bankers: The Wall Street Takeover and Next Financial Meltdown*. New York, NY: Pantheon Books.

Kindleberger, C. P. 1978/2005. *Manias, Panics and Crashes: A History of Financial Crises*. 5th ed. Hoboken, NJ: John Wiley and Sons.

Kindleberger, C. P., E. Despres, and W. S. Salant. 1966. *"The Dollar and World Liquidity: A Minority View,"* the Economist, February 5, C. P. Kindleberger [1981], *International Money: A Collection of Essays*. London: Geroge Allen & Unwin.

Kozak, S., and O. Teplova. 2012. "Securitization as a Tool of Bank Liquidity and Funding Management before and after the Crisis the Case of the EU." *Financial Internet Quarterly: e-Finanse* 8 (4):30–43.

Le Leslé, V. 2012. "Bank debt in Europe: Are Funding Model Broken," *IMF Working Paper Series*, 12/299, December 2012.

Liikanen, E., C. H. Bänziger, J. M. Campa, L. Gallois, M. Goyens, J. P. Krahnen, M. Mazzucchelli, C. Sergeant, Z. Tuma, J. Vanhevel, and H. Wijffels. 2012. High-level Expert Group on Reforming the Structure of the EU Banking Sector: Final Report, Brussels, 2 October 2012.

Maes, S. 2015. "Shadow Banking: A European Perspective." In *Shadow Banking within and across National Borders, World Scientific Studies in International Economics*, edited by S. Claessens, D. Evanoff, G. Kaufman, and L. Laeven, Singapore: World Scientific Publishing, pp. 347–72.

Mallaby, S. 2016. *The Man Who Knew: The Life and Times of Alan Greenspan*. New York, NY: Penguin Press.

McCauley, R. N. 2012. "The Euro and the Yen as Anchor Currencies: before and during the Financial Crisis – Comments on Moss's Paper "The Euro: Internationalised at birth" and Takagi's paper "Internationalising the yen, 1984–2003: Unfinished Agenda or Mission impossible?", Currency Internationalisation: Lessons from the Global Financial Crisis and Prospects for the Future in Asia and the Pacific, *BIS Papers*, No.61, January 2012, pp. 93–104.

McCauley, R. N. 2018. "The 2008 Crisis: Transpacific or Transatlantic?" BIS Quarterly Review 39–58.

Moutot, P., A. Jung, and F. P. Mongelli. 2008. "The Workings of the Eurosystem: Monetary Policy Preparations and Decision-making," *ECB Occasional Paper Series*, No. 79, January 2008.

Nakao, S. 1991/1995. *The Political Economy of Japan Money*. Tokyo: University of Tokyo Press.

Noeth, B., and R. Sengupta. 2012. "Global European Banks and the Financial Crisis," Review, Federal Reserve Bank of St. Louis, November/December 2012, pp. 457–480.

Obstfelt, M. 2009. "Lenders of Last Resort in a Globalized World," Coleman Fung Risk Management Research Center, Institute of Business and Economic Research, UC Berkeley, January 2009.

O'Driscoll, G. P. Jr., 2009. "Money and the Present Crisis." *Cato Journal* 29 (1):167–86.

Papadoa-Schioppa, T. 2000. "EMU and Banking Supervision." In *Which Lender of Last Resort for Europe?*, edited by C.A.E. Goodhart. London: Central Banking Publication, pp.13–29.

Papaioannou, E. and R. Portes. "Costs and Benefits of Running an International Currency," Economic Paper, European Commission, No. 348, November 2008.

Pollard, S. P. 2003. "A Look Inside Two Central Banks: The European Central Bank and the Federal Reserve," *Review*, The Federal Reserve Bank of St. Louis, January/February 2003, pp. 11–30.

Pozsar, Z., T. Adrian, A. Ashcraft, and H. Boesky. 2010. "Shadow Banking," *Federal Reserve Bank of New York working paper*, No.458, July 2010.

Prati, A., and G. J. Schinasi. 1997a. "EMU and International Capital Markets: Structural Implications and Risks." In *EMU and the International Monetary System*, edited by P. R. Masson, T. H. Krueger, and B. G. Turtelboom. Washington DC: IMF, pp. 263–388.

Prati, A., and G. J. Schinasi. 1997b. "European Monetary Union and International Capital Markets: Structural Implications and Risks," *IMF Working paper*, 97/62, May 1997.

Schinasi, G. J., C. F. Kramer, and R. T. Smith. 2001. "Financial Implications of the Shrinking Supply of U.S. Treasury Securities," *IMF working paper*, 01/61, May 2001.

Schinasi, G. J., and P. G. Teixeira. 2006. "The Lender of Last Resort in the European Single Financial Market," *IMF working paper*, 06/127, May 2006.

Shin, H. S. 2010. *Risk and Liquidity*. New York, NY: Oxford University Press.

Shin, H. S. 2012. Global Banking Glut and Loan Risk Premium, Mundell–Fleming Lecture, the 2011 IMF Annual Research Conference, 10–11 November, Princeton University, January 2012.

Singh, M. 2011. "Velocity of Pledged Collateral: Analysis and Implications," *IMF Working Paper*, 11/256, November 2011.

Strange, S. 1986/2016. *Casino Capitalism*. Manchester, UK: Manchester University Press.

Tavlas, G. S., and Y. Ozeki. 1992. "The Internationalization of Currencies: An Appraisal of the Japanese Yen," IMF Occasional Paper, No.90, January 1992.

The Committee on the Global Financial System. 2010. The Role of Margin Requirements and Haircuts in Procyclicality, *CGFS Papers*, No.36, March 2010.

The Committee on the Global Financial System. 2011. Global Liquidity Concept, Measurement and Policy Implication, *CGFS Papers*, No.45, November 2011.

The Financial Crisis Inquiry Commission. 2011. *The Financial Crisis Inquiry Report: Final Report of the National Commission on the Causes of the Financial and Economic Crisis in the United States*. Washington DC: U.S. Government Printing Office.

The Giovannini Group. 1999. "EU Repo Markets: Opportunities for Change," October 1999.

Thiemann, M. 2012. "Out of the Shadow?: Accounting for Special Purpose Entities in European Banking Systems." *Competition and Change* 16 (1):37–55. doi: 10.1179/1024529411Z.0000000003.

Tokunaga, J., and G. Epstein. 2018. "The Endogenous Finance of Global-Dollar Based Financial Fragility in the 2000s: A Minskyan Approach." *Review of Keynesian Economics* 6 (1):62–82. doi: 10.4337/roke.2018.01.04.

White, L. J. 2009. "The Credit Rating Agencies and the Subprime Debacle." *Critical Review* 21 (2–3):389–99. doi: 10.1080/08913810902974964.

Building blocks for the macroeconomics and political economy of housing

Engelbert Stockhammer and Christina Wolf

ABSTRACT
Housing played an essential part in the global financial crisis 2007–2008 and the Euro crisis. Large parts of bank lending continue to go to mortgages. Housing wealth is the largest part of wealth for most households and is, at the same time, more dispersed than other forms of wealth. House prices exhibit pronounced fluctuations that are closely linked to credit growth. Housing thus plays a crucial role in the macro-economy, which has become even more pronounced under neoliberalism. We scrutinize different theoretical approaches to housing. Despite its theoretical shortcomings, mainstream economics has pioneered empirical research on wealth effects in consumption and recently documented the role of house prices in financial cycles. Post-Keynesian theory emphasizes endogenous money creation, cycles in asset prices and debt, and has formalized the notion of a debt-driven demand regime. Comparative political economy research has recently developed the concept of the varieties of residential capital-ism, which has different structures of house ownership and housing finance at the core of political coalitions. Marxist pol-itical economy has long established the intrinsic link between ownership of land and economic rent and notes that home-ownership can act as force of working-class fragmentation. Wealth surveys can be used to trace the extent of conflicting interests in a class-relational approach.

Introduction

Housing is an oddly underresearched topic in macroeconomics and polit-ical economy. This does not mean there is no research on housing. Quite the contrary, there are subfields like real estate and housing economics or urban studies that have long paid close attention to issues of housing. But these constitute specialized fields. This may be changing as housing and mortgage finance have gained prominence after the 2008 crisis, in which mortgages played a central role. However, in most baseline macroeconomic models, including the mainstream versions as well as the Post-Keynesian (PK) or Marxist versions, there is no housing market. This is surprising, given that housing accounts for 30 to 50 percent of a household's expenditures and around 90 percent of household debt, and residential investment constitutes approximately half of total investment. Similarly, in political economy, admittedly a heterogeneous field, there was until recently little systematic incorporation of housing. The extensive debates on class analysis, for instance, have sidestepped the issue of working-class homeownership.

In the global financial crisis (GFC) of 2008 and the Euro crisis, housing and housing finance, of course, have played a key role: Real estate bubbles were a key factor for the booms that preceded the crisis, derivatives on mortgages and, in particular, subprime mortgage securities were at the epicenter of the early stages of the crisis, and their price collapse drove hedge funds into bankruptcy, ultimately paralyzing the shadow banking sector and eventually the entire financial system. Although in Europe the subprime securitization featured less prominently, the house price booms and busts in Ireland and Spain were severe. In Great Britain, the bankruptcy of Northern Rock was due to its aggressive growth, mostly in mortgages. Thus, since the crisis of 2008 there has been a strong growth in interest in the role of housing and housing finance, and a reconsideration of the how financial systems operate more generally.

The GFC has led to dynamically growing analyses of the various impacts of housing and housing finance, ranging from historical analyses of the composition of credit (Jordà, Schularick, and Taylor 2016), the impact of housing wealth vs. financial wealth on consumption expenditures, the impact of housing vs. business credit on growth (Bezemer 2014; Bezemer, Grydaki, and Zhang 2016), and analyses of the drivers of household debt (Stockhammer and Wildauer 2016) to housing in political economy (Aalbers and Christophers 2014a).

This article surveys a rapidly growing literature in the field of macroeconomics and political economy of housing and housing finance. The aim, first, is to review the literature on the impact of housing, mortgages, and real estate prices on macroeconomic growth and stability and to assess to what extent different economic paradigms can account for the stylized facts. Second, we review the literature on the impact of housing structures on political attitudes and class structures and assess how different approaches can explain these. Third, we apply a class-based analysis to the U.K. Wealth and Asset Survey with the aim to delineate a future empirical research agenda combining political economy and macroeconomic approaches.

Our review suggests the following stylized facts that different theories have to explain: Mortgages are the largest components of household debt.

Real estate prices reveal both increases over the last decades and a cyclical pattern, with a cycle length well beyond regular business cycles. Changes in household debt have become important drivers of growth, and the level of household debt is a predictor of the severity of recessions. Periods of rising house prices often do not come with a spread of homeownership, implying that the increase in house prices will have distributional effects. There is some evidence that homeownership impacts political attitudes, in particular regarding the welfare state. Homeownership is strongly related to income distribution.

The article is structured as follows: The next section discusses analyses of housing and housing finance from economic and financial history. We then survey the contributions of mainstream economics and post-Keynesian theory on the topic. Then we review models of house price cycles, and cover comparative and Marxist political economy. Next we discuss the housing in the United Kingdom from a class-analytic perspective, before we conclude.

Economic and financial history

Although economic history has long-standing concern for corporate finance, in particular, the finance of industrialization most financial histories do not cover housing finance. Kindleberger's (1993) seminal *Financial History of Western Europe* has several index entries for mortgages, but these refer mostly to agricultural mortgages rather than household credit. Similarly, in one of the early books on financialization, Arrighi (1994) took a long historical view, in which financialization features in the long downswing of the hegemonic power losing industrial leadership but maintaining financial dominance. He discussed industrial finance and government debt, but not household debt or mortgages.

It is only recently that more systematic histories of housing and housing finance have been written. These point to at least three important shifts in housing finance and house price dynamics, which need to be explained by macroeconomic and political economy theories. First, Blackwell and Kohl (2018) and Kohl (2018) gave an overview of the history of mortgage credit institutions. These differ in important ways from the banks that deal with businesses. In particular the market/bank-based distinction does not apply in this form to mortgages. The Scandinavian and Germanic countries developed forms of mortgage securitization that allowed specialized institutions to emerge that sold on mortgages in the form of covered bonds—that is, they remained on the banks' balance sheets.

Jordà, Schularick, and Taylor (2016) documented the secular increase in mortgage lending as share of bank balance sheets. They reported declining share of mortgages as share of total bank lending until World War I, an increasing share in the interwar period that consequently collapsed, and then a sustained rise of mortgage credit after World War II, which accelerated after 1980. Whereas in 1900 around one-third of loans were nonmortgages, by 2000 the share was two-thirds (Jordà, Schularick, and Taylor 2016: Figure 4).

Knoll, Schularick, and Steger (2017) presented data on real house prices, which show that, fluctuation notwithstanding, real house prices were relatively stable until World War II and began a secular increase (with larger fluctuations) after the war. The following sections review the ability of different approaches to macroeconomics and political economy to account for both the emergence of these trends and their effects.

Mainstream macroeconomics

Mainstream macroeconomics has lacked a systematic treatment of debt and assets. At the core this is related to the strong role of assumptions of rationality and life cycle optimization behavior. This is has ruled out interest in speculative asset prices movement and often has resulted in a separation of the discussion of financial and "real" issues. Real issues are about technology shocks, which give the impetus for real business cycle theory (RBC) and are still at the core of modern DSGE model, which are essentially RBC models with nominal rigidities. The assumption of rationality and perfect foresight also ruled out an analysis of bankruptcies.

In the background of these models is a loanable funds theory of financial markets, in which lending is understood as a use of saving, and saving a (positive) function of the interest rate. This is at odds with Keynesian understanding (saving depending on income) and modern theories of endogenous money creation (in which loans create deposits). It also focuses on net lending and tends to regard households as the surplus (saving) unit and firms as the deficit (borrowing) unit. In fact, the lending boom of the 2000s was driven by household borrowing (and financial sector borrowing) and was gross lending.

The neoclassical literature on housing is theoretically uninteresting. Housing is seen as a "standard commodity" (Fallis 1985: 34), the demand for which is determined by relative prices of other goods and households' budget constraint stemming from their labor–leisure tradeoff. The supply of housing follows a standard Cobb-Douglas production function, land being one among other capital inputs and paid at its marginal product. Investment decisions, then, reflect producers' time discount rate (equal to the market rate of interest), and price is determined by the forces of demand and supply (Fallis 1985).

Mainstream macroeconomics is divided into new classical and new Keynesian streams. The new Keynesian approach accepts the need for microfoundations based on optimizing behavior, but questions whether markets are always clearing given market imperfections like transaction costs and asymmetric information. That gave rise to Stiglitz and Weiss's (1981) model of credit rationing, which is still a benchmark model and informs the financial accelerator model (Bernanke, Gertler, and Gilchrist 1999). The Stiglitz model, notably, is a model of rationing *credit to businesses*—that is, it is about corporate credit, not mortgages. The financial accelerator model and the related lending channel literature have emphasized that net worth will affect the value of collateral and thus access to credit. Therefore, banks will want to restrict lending if they have balance sheet problems. In the new Keynesian setting (i.e., with information asymmetries), credit constraints matter for macroeconomic outcomes. In an NK Dynamic Stochastic General Equilibrium (DSGE) model with two types of households that differ by their rate of time preference, Eggertsson and Krugman (2012) showed that episodes of what they referred to a "Minsky Koo debt deflation" can arise, but the model has no proper financial sector, and financial crises are not endogenous.

However, despite the theoretical limitations of the mainstream models, mainstream policy institutions did generate a substantial amount of empirically or policy-driven research. In particular, central banks and the OECD were leading the empirical literature on wealth effects (Boone, Giorno, and Richardson 1998; IMF 2000). This literature was motivated in the 1990s by the declining saving rate of U.S. households, which from a neoclassical perspective would depress long-run growth (Maki and Palumbo 2001). In the 1990s, however, it came with relatively high levels of growth. A sizable literature emerged that highlighted the role of increasing wealth as a cause of increasing consumption. Initially, the focus was on financial wealth and equity prices in particular, as the 1990s were a period of sustained equity price inflation, which eventually ended in the dot.com crash of 2000. However, although equity prices collapsed in 2000 and remained subdued thereafter, consumption expenditures held up, which led to the realization that housing wealth is typically (at least in the Anglo-Saxon countries) more important for consumption, as homeownership is widespread and real estate is good collateral (Case, Shiller, and Quigley 2005; Slacalek 2009).

That said, the empirical literature on wealth effects fits somewhat uneasily within the rational foresight model, which is reflected in that literature. First, it is not clear whether housing wealth in such a model is wealth at all (Buiter 2010). Second, there is a tension between theory and the empirical approach in these articles. In their theory sections, the empirical wealth

effects articles refer to rational actor/perfect foresight models and then esti-
mate consumption equations that react *to market prices*. In other words,
perfectly rational individuals in, say, Ireland, observe a sharp increase in
real estate prices and act on it as if it were a fundamental increase in real
estate values—that is, the perfectly rational individuals never worry about
the possibility of a bubble even in the face of spectacular price increases.

Especially after the crisis there was an assessment of the impact of real
estate prices on credit availability. Among the most impressive of these was
a series of articles by Mian and Sufi, who used fine-grained survey data to
document how the decline in house prices affected U.S. households across
regions (Mian, Rao, and Sufi 2013) and argued that credit supply shocks
explain much of the housing bubble (Mian and Sufi 2018). Several authors
at the critical edge of the new Keynesian mainstream have made the case
that lending and house prices can reinforce each other to give rise to bubbles (Goodhart and Hofmann 2008; Muellbauer 2007), without, however,
turning this into a full theory of endogenous cycles.

Since the crisis, it is fair to say, this critical research on financial instability and the long-term growth impact of finance has turned into a sizeable
stream, even if it presses ahead without adequate theory. Aizenman and
Jinjarak (2014) provided evidence that capital flows have a powerful effect
on real estate prices (see also Badarinza and Ramadorai 2018). Arcand,
Berkes, and Panizza (2015) provided evidence that finance has negative
effects on growth beyond a certain threshold—namely, when private debt
reaches 100 percent of GDP. This represents a major departure from the
dominant view that financial deepening has a positive impact on growth
(Levine 1997). Borio (2012) and Barrell and colleagues (2010) documented
that house price inflation is a leading indicator for financial crises.
Drehman, Borio, and Tsatsaronis (2012) and Aikman, Haldane, and Nelson
(2015) provided evidence for the existence of financial cycles, which is
inconsistent with the notion that financial crises are due to exogenous
shocks. These financial cycles are longer than regular business cycles.

What emerges from this brief survey of mainstream economics is a tension between a theoretical framework that, with its rationality and market
clearing assumptions, is ill-suited to explain recent dynamics and crises
emanating from the real estate sector and, at the same time, a dynamic
empirical research program that bypasses the rigidities of the theoretical framework.

Post-Keynesian economics

Post-Keynesian economics (PKE) does not employ the lifetime optimizing
assumptions of neoclassical economics. Rather, it assumes given marginal

propensities of consumption that will differ by class position or by the position within the income distribution. To some extent, PKE has suffered from the relatively independent advancement of its Kaleckian and Minskyan stream. As the basic Keynesian model assumes autonomous consumption, this implies that if there are demand shocks—of which there are plenty in a Keynesian economy—parts of the population (presumably the poor or those with illiquid assets) will have to accumulate debt in order to accommodate to the resulting income declines while autonomous consumption stays constant. Despite the fact that there is a logical role for household borrowing in PKE, it has not traditionally played an important role. Nor has housing. The PKE class model seems to implicitly have been interpreted as one in which workers not only do not have property in the means of production but also none in the means of reproduction, which includes housing. We will return to this issue later. Wealth effects do not feature prominently in PKE (until the development of SFC models), as they were historically associated with the neoclassical and monetarist criticisms of Keynesianism.

There are five debates in which household debt and ultimately housing do enter. First, Palley (1994) and Dutt (2006) proposed models of working-class household debt. The poor are borrowing from the rich, which will have positive short-term effects on consumption (as finance is made available to those with high marginal consumption propensities), but negative longer term effects, as interest payments distribute income toward those with high savings propensities. These models are focused on consumer debt and do not treat housing explicitly.

Second, an important innovation in PKE has been the development of stock flow consistent (SFC) models. These track all flows and stocks in a macroeconomic model and enforce consistency between the two. In these models, economic sectors are thought of in a balance sheet context, and assets and liabilities will enter behavioral equations.

Godley and Tobin have pioneered these models, and Godley has repeatedly highlighted that economies are anchored in stock-flow norms. If one assumes that consumption depends on disposable income and some measure of wealth, this implies that households will attempt to reach a target wealth-to-income ratio (Godley and Lavoie 2007: 75). If wealth increases beyond the target ratio, households will consume that "excess wealth." As housing wealth is the most important wealth component for households, borrowing in order to realize real estate capital gains would be the result. Indeed, Godley (1999) warned early that rising U.S. household debt would be unsustainable.

Third, in the demand regimes literature, which began as an operationalization of the Bhaduri-Marglin framework, there was a recognition that some of the actual neoliberal growth models were relying heavily on the growth of household debt, which fueled consumption growth (Lavoie and Stockhammer 2013; Stockhammer 2012). Although some authors have suggested that rising income inequality has been the main driver of household debt (Kapeller and Schütz 2014; Perugini, Hölscher, and Collie 2016), Stockhammer and Wildauer (2016) presented evidence that real estate prices are the main cause.

Fourth, although Minsky (1978) focused on business debt rather than household debt, the notion of endogenous financial instability has also been applied to the household sector. Ryoo (2016) presented a model of housing cycles that is driven by nonlinear expectation of house price inflation (such as in Dieci and Westerhoff 2012).

Fifth, with close reference to the financialization debates (see below), several authors have suggested that increased lending in the neoliberal era would result in higher volatility rather than higher growth. Bezemer and colleagues (2016) analyzed lending decisions of banks and highlighted the distinction between nonfinancial credit and asset market credit. Real estate transactions are an example for the latter (but it also includes credit to financial institutions). Bezemer and colleagues (2016) argued that the two types of credit have different demand and growth effects. Arestis and González (2014) was one of the few PK articles that explicitly modeled the housing sector in a macro model. They proposed a model of the supply and demand for housing based on PK endogenous money theory. The model allows for private sector borrowing derived from real estate transactions; however, it does not explicitly model business and household borrowing decisions separately.

We found that PKE, with it basis in conventional behavior and procyclical animal spirits and its theory of endogenous money creation, is better equipped to analyze financial cycles and crisis, but it has been slow to apply this framework to housing. There are several noteworthy, rigorous, empirical studies on debt-driven growth models and the differential impact of business credit and mortgage and financial credit, but overall PKE has not translated into an empirical research program on housing.

Models of house price cycles

Overall it is surprising how few macroeconomic models of house price cycles there are. There is strong evidence of financial cycles (Aikman et al 2015; Drehman, Borio, and Tsatsaronis 2012), which typically have found that house prices are a key component of these cycles. Glaeser (2013) documented the long history of real estate speculation in the United States. House price inflation also performs well in tests of early warning systems for financial crises (Barrell et al. 2010). The positive feedback loop between house prices and credit is well established (e.g., Arestis and González 2014). But still, given that most macro models fail to include the housing sector, even fewer model house price cycles, with some exceptions that are grounded in PKE, behavioral economics or heterogeneous agents modeling.

Dieci and Westerhoff (2012) presented a model of the housing market in which endogenous price cycles emerge from the interaction of actors with fundamentalist and those with momentum-based expectations; however, they did not offer a full macroeconomic model. On the PKE side, Ryoo (2016) presented a model in which households form extrapolative expectations about house price increases and use increased borrowing to finance consumption, which drives the boom. Assuming a nonlinear expectation function eventually the bubble bursts. Bofinger and colleagues (2013) extended a NK DSGE model with a monetary policy rule to include a housing market. They built on De Grauwe (2012), who introduced fundamentalists momentum trader dynamics in a full macro model with heuristics and learning. Bofinger and colleagues (2013) applied this to the housing sector and showed that the fundamentalist momentum trader interactions can generate cycles.

Although house price cycles can be modeled, changing trends over time—such as the increase in mortgages as share of bank lending or increases in the frequency and magnitude of house price fluctuations observed by economic historians—call for an incorporation of political and institutional factors. This bridge is offered by political economy approaches. The next two sections review comparative political economy (CPE) and Marxist political economy approaches to housing, respectively.

Comparative political economy and the financialization debates

CPE is an emerging field that is informed both by economics—in particular, the classical school and Keynesian traditions—and by social sciences—in particular, political science (Clift 2014). Finance and housing have not featured centrally in this field until recently.

Within CPE the varieties of capitalism (VoC) model has been particularly influential because it managed to integrate previous insights in the differences in labor relations, welfare systems, and financial systems. It emphasizes substantial differences in national capitalisms. The central reference point in establishing those varieties of capitalism is how they achieve competitiveness. The most famous distinction of VoC is between liberal and coordinated market economies. The focus on competitiveness has implied a focus on corporate finance (as opposed to housing finance) and a functionalism (the financial sector is analyzed as providing finance for business rather than being the origin as financial crises). The widely used distinction within financial systems between market- and bank-based systems stems from the analysis of corporate finance.

Some of the CPE literature does not adhere to the VoC framework and gets closer to PK growth models, showing that credit growth sustains demand regimes and welfare provision increasingly relies on housing and housing finance. Crouch (2009) coined the term "privatized Keynesianism," arguing that original Keynesianism relied on government intervention and thus public debt to stabilize the economy and consumers' expectations. This has, since the 1980s, been replaced by a regime, in which credit is provided to household by commercial banks and other lenders. Crouch cited rising levels of mortgage debt as evidence and argued that in some countries—namely, the United Kingdom—this turned into an effective policy regime, but he did not offer a systematic comparative analysis. Crouch did not discuss the fact that private lending tends to be procyclical (in contrast to Keynesian deficit spending, which is countercyclical) but highlighted that "financial firms and entrepreneurs developed forms of knowledge that encouraged eventually self-destructive decisions" (Crouch 2009: 393).

Watson (2010) made a similar argument and used the term "house price Keynesianism," which (again, for the United Kingdom) he situated in the context of a move toward asset-based welfare. Watson (2010) analyzed the impact of house prices and mortgage debt on the subjectivity and identity of households and also highlighted the cyclical nature of house prices.

Parts of the CPE literature have emphasized political implications of homeownership. Schwartz and Seabrooke (2008) proposed a theory of varieties of residential capitalism. Unlike the original VoC approach, competitiveness is not a reference point in their analysis (presumably because the national housing markets do not compete internationally). Rather, they offered a rich classification of the political economy of homeownership and housing finance. Based on the systems of housing finance and homeownership rates, they distinguished between corporatist (high mortgage debt and low ownership: Germany, the Netherlands, Denmark), liberal (high mortgage rates and high ownership: the United Kingdom, the United States, Australia, Norway), statist developmentalist (low mortgage and low ownership: Austria, France, Japan, Sweden) and Catholic-familial (low mortgage and high ownership: Belgium, Italy, Ireland, Spain). They emphasized the political economy implication of these regimes: Home ownership tends to undermine the viability of large welfare states, in particular, public pension systems (the requirement of high down payment conflicts with the ability to pay higher taxes); high ownership rates will make it more difficult to find majorities to pass rent control laws and provide public housing. This was confirmed by Ansell (2014), who, based on U.S. and U.K, survey data, found econometric evidence that homeownership in the presence of house price appreciation is negatively correlated to individual preferences for redistribution and social insurance systems. Yet, Schwartz and Seabrooke's (2008) analysis was static in describing the interaction of housing structures and political majorities as well as some institutional complementarities. In contrast, financial crises or house prices cycles do not feature.

Blackwell and Kohl (2018) provided a history of housing finance. They offered a classification based on the distinction a deposit-based bank system, a mortgage bond-based bank system, state-based, and a peer-based lending system. They provided historical evidence and a historical explanation, which extended Gerschenkron's theory of late industrialisers, but with quite different results. In particular they argued that some patterns of corporate finance are inverted for housing finance. The early industrializers developed deposit-based mortgages—that is, a form of bank-based systems. In contrast, latecomers like Scandinavian and Germanic countries developed a form of mortgage finance that is more market-based in that it relies on mortgage securitization. Extreme latecomers typically relied on state-based systems. Kohl (2018) argued that higher mortgages do not necessarily lead to higher homeownership rates based on a historical review since the late 19th century and econometric analysis for the postwar period. Thus mortgage growth is neither necessary nor sufficient for homeownership. Kohl, more than the other CPE literature, spoke directly to the cyclical nature of house prices and the house price-mortgage debt loop.

In the financialization debates, issues of housing come relatively late—that is, in the 1990s. Initial debates on financialization focused on financial liberalization, in particular in developing economies, and on corporate governance and shareholder value orientation—that is, the financialization of businesses rather than households. These emphasized the potentially negative effects of financialization on growth and the business cycle and its distributional implications. However, by the late 1990s and early 2000s, the financialization of households and the rise of household debt featured more prominently. Langley (2007) highlighted the changing subjectivities stemming from the increased financial involvement of households. These include, in particular, the rise of mortgages and private pension provision. Erturk and Solari (2007) highlighted the shift in bank balance sheet from lending to businesses toward lending to households (i.e., mortgages) and fee generating activities (i.e., investment banking activities). Changing historical trends in housing markets observed by economic historians are thus located in the wider phenomenon of financialization by this stream of literature.

Much like in macroeconomics, housing has been a side issue until recently. In the last few years, research on housing has left the VoC framework behind and investigated the political impact of homeownership—in particular, on attitudes toward the welfare state and the pension systems—and borrowed from Keynesian analyses of debt. A core tenet of CPE rests on the two-way relationship between housing and policy regimes: Housing and housing finance systems are shaped by policy regimes, and policy regimes are themselves influenced if not reducible to housing interests. Although there are several useful contributions a unified CPE approach to housing is not yet discernible.

Marxist political economy

Marxist political economy approaches the question of how and to what extent housing has restructured systemic dynamics of accumulation through conflicting interest around ownership of land and real estate and the mediation of these conflicts through the state and through the market. As for the other schools of thought, it is striking that housing appears in niche debates rather than constituting an integral part of their core theory (such as in Shaikh 2016). The theorization of social relations of land ownership builds on the concept of land rents and power of land/property owners to extract payment from nonowners (Aalbers and Christophers 2014a, 2014b; Berry 2014). Debates over the origin of land rent in the urban context are theoretically unsettled (Basu 2018; Harvey 1974; Park 2014). Yet, there are a number of points of agreement—in particular, the collective nature underlying increases in land values—the value of land being enhanced, for instance, by public spending on infrastructure, or ultimately collective processes like the emergence of production agglomerations or urbanization processes more widely (Harvey 1974).

The conceptualization of housing around rent allows for two things. First, it establishes contradictions of wealth accumulation based on rent appropriation. Rent is a benefit derived from the exclusive possession of a factor of production in excess of the production cost of that factor, and is therefore an unearned windfall income to be distinguished from productive activity and profits (Ryan-Collins, Lloyd, and MacFarlane 2017). The value of land not being directly related to investment the owner of land has put in the land but, instead, determined socially, making ownership over this scarce if manmade asset a means of rent extraction.

If hardly proposing a new insight, Marxists are more explicit about the fact that housing and land cannot form a long-term basis for wealth accumulation. For value to be appropriated it has to be created somewhere and, as Harvey (1974: 241) noted, "If all capital chases rent and no capital goes into production, then no value will be produced out of which the transfer payment that rent represents can come." In the Marxist reading, for capital gains to be realized on land and real estate, prices of land and real estate have to rise faster than the general price level. Because rising house prices will eventually be passed down into rents, rents paid by tenants will rise faster than inflation and wages (Berry 1986; Edel 1982). Increases in disposable income outright owners enjoy in the absence of rent payments rely on the same conditions. This, in turn, implies limits to property-based wealth accumulation and wealth effects.

Second, it allows establishing class interests opposed to one another. Ownership of housing and real estate can be related to the appearance of conflicting housing-related interests, which cross-cut basic class divisions. Classes in the orthodox Marxist reading are understood as antagonistic interests between workers and capitalists, other struggles being contained within and organized around these boundaries. The concrete manifestations of interests, class tactics, and alliances cannot, however, be mechanically derived from these two abstract categories but will depend on particular historical conjunctures expressed politically and ideologically (Poulantzas 1982). An important element in tracing the concrete manifestations of interests and potential alliances with sections of other classes is the process of class fragmentation. Class fragmentation can have different origins, but a limited number of contributions identify housing as an important driver of working-class fragmentation (Berry 1986; Harvey 1982). Whereas Saunders (1984) treated housing-related interests as undermining the usefulness of the capital Labor divide, Berry pointed out that access to owner-occupation is income determined and therefore itself determined by labor market outcomes. When fragmentation occurs within classes, this can generate significant income inequalities within classes and lead to overlap in income levels across class boundaries. This does not necessarily mean that common interests transcending traditional class boundaries form, but there is likely going to be intraclass conflict to protect and extend these income shares. Therefore, the promotion of property ownership among workers ultimately serves capitalists in that it establishes workers' allegiance with the principle of private property (Harvey 1982) and can drive homeowners to defend their privileged position in the workplace against the interests of other workers (Berry 1986).

Harvey (1974) located housing-related class interests in conflicting interests between landlords and low-income tenants as well as between speculator-developers and middle classes. He emphasized that the balance of power between these different classes needs to be examined together with supportive political institutions. The state—following multiple sets of logic, often at the same time—plays a crucial role in creating, recreating, changing, and restricting development of housing markets, thereby tipping the balance of power between different housing-related interest groups.

Both CPE and Marxist political economy provide important bridges to other social sciences that help account for institutional and political factors behind observed correlations between housing and macroeconomic aggregates and changes to trends over time. CPE has been successful in establishing patterns from a comparative perspective, documenting the complementarity of homeownership and welfare regimes, and elaborating political aspects of debt-driven growth models. A distinctive feature of Marxist approaches is that they regard social outcomes as shaped by class structures and conflict based in production relations. Homeownership thus represents a fragmentation of the working class, which impacts its bargaining position. However, Marxists have been slow to take this class- and rents-based approach to housing forward empirically in terms of linking it to political attitudes and macroeconomic dynamics.

Exploring housing in a class-relational approach based on wealth survey: An illustration from the United Kingdom

To illustrate the relevance of these points (i.e., contradiction of rent-based accumulation and conflicting housing-related interests) but also the challenges in taking these points forward empirically, we briefly turn to the example of the United Kingdom. Here, several housing-related policy shifts have promoted real estate as a means of wealth accumulation, investment opportunity, and insurance against dwindling wages, pensions, and welfare provision. These policy shifts had a substantial impact on macroeconomic outcomes, including household debt, house prices, and financial instability (Fernandez and Aalbers 2017). Yet, they also contributed to the appearance of conflicting housing-related interests, which cross-cut basic class divisions and changed the accumulation dynamics among firms.

First, from the early 1980s onward U.K. housing policy shifted away from subsidies for the supply side through state-sponsored housing development toward demand-side incentives with the aim of helping individuals to either buy or rent (Ryan-Collins, Lloyd, and MacFarlane 2017). Second, since the late 1970s around half of the United Kingdom's public estate was privatized, equivalent to 10 percent of British land mass (Christophers 2018). Finally, financial deregulation was a significant counterpart of the Thatcher government's promotion of demand for owner-occupied housing as a means to widen access to private mortgage finance (Hasan and Taghavi 2002; Wood 2018).

These policy shifts have strengthened class interests emphasized by Harvey (1974), in particular, those of speculator developers tied to finance capital and those of landlords more generally. They favored monopolization and speculation in the developer market, smaller developers being driven out of the market as social house building no longer acted as counter-cyclical force to the business cycle. The release of public land, in turn, served larger developers to engage in speculative land banking (Christophers 2018). The growth in the supply of houses reduced substantially, annual housing completion being less than half its peak in 1968 by 2013. This, coupled with increased demand, acted as a driver of substantial house price increases in the United Kingdom since the late 1980s (Ryan-Collins, Lloyd, and MacFarlane 2017). Private landlordism increased since the 1990s and intensified after the GFC (Kemp 2015) becoming, in fact, a wealth-accumulation strategy (Soaita et al. 2017).

The housing related policy shifts are also likely to have contributed to working-class fragmentation into nonproperty-owning working class and property-owning working class, as theorized by Berry (1986). Based on the first five waves of the UK Wealth and Asset Survey (WAS; Office For National Statistics, Social Survey Division 2018), Arundel (2017) has empirically established housing as the major driver of wealth inequality in the United Kingdom. The WAS can be taken further to trace inequalities specifically in a class-relational approach, treating them as coming out of antagonistic interests between and within classes, mirroring an approach pioneered by Fessler and Schürz (2018). This can serve as a starting point to map the potential importance of antagonistic housing-related interests within classes.

Fessler and Schürz (2018) distinguished between renters, owners, and capitalists. They maintained that these ownership structures imply unequal power relationships between classes and drive inequality, with a clear concentration of renters in the first three deciles of the income distribution, a concentration of owners between the fourth and eighth deciles, and a concentration of capitalists among the two wealthiest deciles both in the United States and in the Euroarea.

However, different ways to delineate intraclass fragmentation and conflict are possible. In what follows, we define housing-related class fragmentation as antagonistic interests between renters, outright owners, mortgage owners, and rentiers, including the latter to account for the Marxist emphasis on rents emanating from housing. Renters are all those who report to rent their main residence.[1] Outright owners are those who report owning their main residence without a mortgage and do not derive any rental income. Mortgage owners are those who report owning their main residence with a mortgage but do not derive any rental income from other property. Rentiers own their main residence with or without a mortgage and also own other land or real estate, such as buy-to-let properties, from which they derive rental income.

Owner-occupiers have an interest in increasing house prices to realize capital gains on their property wealth. Yet, property values being loosely correlated to rent prices, this is diametrically opposed to the interests of renters. Politically, this could play out in opposing interests around new housing development. Although not explicitly pursuing a Marxist class-relational approach, Coelho and colleagues (2017) traced political conflict between homeowners and voters with interests in social housing. Vested interests of existing homeowners for prices increase influence planning decisions, the housing stock growing significantly less in local authorities with higher proportions of owner-occupiers among local households.

Mortgage owners have, in principle, similar interests to those of outright owners, although their behavior in the workplace might be very different. Mortgage owners depend on bank finance and are, in the face of rising house prices, heavily dependent on keeping their employment and also to remaining in high-paid positions (Kim, Tadeu Lima, and Setterfield 2017). Harvey (1982) saw this as the ultimate way to discipline workers' militancy. They are thus likely to be ready to defend their privileged positions in the workplace, possibly against the interests of nonproperty-owning workers. The outright-owning working class, by contrast, is to an extent decommodified by housing wealth, notably through the higher disposable income they enjoy in the absence of rent payments. Finally, rentiers rely for a part of their income on rental income. They therefore have an active interest for there to be a pool of (low-income) tenants with no alternative to private renting. This is likely to be mirrored in an opposition to social housing but could also be expressed in support for precarious forms of employment like zero-hour contracts.

Table 1 summarizes the proportions of these different tenure classes within the sample. The WAS (Office For National Statistics, Social Survey Division 2018) surveyed 18,611 households, which with appropriate weights add up to 25.6 million households, hence representing the total number of households in the United Kingdom. Of these, 32.7 percent are renters. Outright owners and mortgage owners account for roughly 30 percent of households each. Finally, there are a nonnegligible number of U.K. households who derive rental income from property, in total 1.6 million households (i.e., 6.4 percent of households).

Table 1. Distribution of tenure types in the United Kingdom, 2014–2016.

	No. observations (sample size)	Weighted no. of observations (population size)	% of total population
Total	18,611	25,602,086	100
Renter	4,688	8,381,300	32.7
Owner-outright	7,467	7,835,424	30.2
Owner-mortgage	4,777	7,750,106	29.9
Rentier	1,679	1,635,256	6.4

Note. Calculations based on Wealth and Assets Survey, Wave 5, 2014–2016.

It is noteworthy that mortgage owners and rentiers are overrepresented in managerial and professional occupations. This is particularly pronounced for rentiers, 62 percent of whom report pursuing managerial occupations. By contrast, renters are overrepresented in routine and manual occupations (50 percent), although roughly one-third of outright owners also report pursuing or having pursued this type of profession (Table A1 in the Appendix). Yet, 88 percent of outright owners are older than 55. By contrast, 65 percent of renters, 81 percent of mortgage owners, and 52 percent of rentiers are younger than 55 (Table A2).

We find substantial differences in total annual household income, employment income, and pensions between the different housing statuses, mean income being lowest among renters (£23,465), followed by outright owners (£32,214). The highest average annual incomes emerge among the rentiers (£63,479). Note that although these differences are driven by labor market outcomes (employment income of rentiers, for instance, being nearly twice that of outright owners and around three times that of renters when excluding pensioners), income from rent accounts for substantial parts of income of rentiers. Average annual rental incomes of rentiers (£13,061) are in the same order of magnitude as renters' average employee incomes (£12,861; see Table 2). Rental incomes represent 41 percent of rentiers' of employee incomes (31 percent when excluding pensioners) and 21 percent of their total average annual income. Notice that these rental incomes largely exceed any income derived from investment, rental incomes being around four times higher than investment income (calculations based on Table 2). In short, there appears to be a group of high-income earners who actively play the housing market and derive substantial parts of their total income from rental payments.

This allows for three observations. First, we note that housing outcomes are correlated with income level and occupational groupings, which supports class-analytic approaches. The fact that housing outcomes appear to be correlated to labor market outcomes raises the question of causality. It can be interpreted as housing outcomes reflecting capital–labor relations (as in Berry 1986). Yet, in line with Fessler and Schürz (2018), housing outcomes may also reinforce inequality through rent payments received by rentiers, capital gains, and availability of housing capital and collateral. Second, homeownership is widespread, which implies that substantial parts of the working class are homeowner. This poses some challenges for Marxists approaches that originally conceived the working class without substantial wealth (and thus forced to sell their labor power), but it makes arguments of class segmentations more relevant. Third, an open question is whether there is a real anchor for house prices (and thus capital gains), or whether they are driven by financial factors and speculative dynamics.

Table 2. Average income by tenure type.

	Tot. inc.[a]	Emp. inc.[b]	Emp. inc. (ex. pen.)[c]	Inc. rent[d]	Inc. invst.[e]
Renter	23,465	12,861	14,319	54	195
Owner-mortgage	43,860	35,972	37,568	0	509
Owner-outright	32,214	10,954	23,308	0	2,391
Rentier	63,479	32,031	42,702	13,061	3,272

Notes. Calculations based on Wealth and Assets Survey, Wave 5, 2014–2016.
aMean household total regular annual income;
bmean household annual employment income;
cmean household annual employment income, excluding pensioners;
dmean household annual income from rent;
emean household annual income from investment.

From a Marxist viewpoint, for increases in capital gains on real estate to occur, rents paid by tenants must rise faster than prices and wages. This implies a limit to how far property prices can rise and hence limits to housing-based wealth accumulation. In contrast, in the PK view, expectations about the future and credit availability are the key factors determining real estate prices. That implies that there is no real anchor, but cyclical speculative dynamics.

In the course of the last boom, the system pushed toward social limits. Strikingly, for private renters in the lowest two income deciles, net rent (excluding utility payments) constitutes 41 percent and 37 percent of households' disposable income, respectively (see Table 3).[2] These figures increase to 57 percent and 45 percent when including utilities payments (see Table A4). By contrast, outright owners spend only between 5 percent and 23 percent on housing-related costs. Hence, the implications of owning versus renting a home on household budget are substantial.

The challenge remains to establish antagonistic interests empirically, not just conceptually. From the above, we identify the following open empirical questions. First, how does working-class fragmentation play out in the workplace, and how does it translate into political attitudes? Second, how do shifting class relations (working-class fragmentation and strengthening of rentiers) correlate to macroeconomic aggregates—namely, debt and consumption? How do the antagonistic interests between renters and rentiers play out politically and ideologically?

Indeed, empirical scholarship on housing-related class interests is scarce. The emphasis so far has been on discourse and social norms rather than on capital–labor relations. Wood (2018) demonstrated that housing-related institutional shifts have created structural conditions that shape agency by transforming private homeownership and mortgage-led accumulation into a dominant social norm in the United Kingdom. Hancock and Mooney (2013) showed that the working class relying on social housing is stigmatized in the United Kingdom, their reliance on social housing said to be

Table 3. Net rent as share of normal household weekly disposable income, 2016–2017.

Decile	Renter-private (percentages)	Renter-social (percentages)
1 (poorest)	41	13
2	37	10
3	28	13
4	24	12
5	26	14
6	26	11
7	21	13
8	19	9
9	21	9
10 (richest)	21	5

Note. Calculations based on U.K. Living Costs and Food Survey, 2016–2017.

the consequence of irresponsible and disorderly behavior, which serves to regulate and control working-class communities.

Conclusion

So far housing has been given little consideration in the core of macroeconomics and political economy. This is despite growing evidence of the importance of housing for economic activity and, in particular, the central role of household and mortgage debt for financial crises. But even in normal (i.e., noncrisis) times, housing-related expenditures constitute a large amount of household budget and around half of residential investment. Housing has been explored in subfields and academic niches.

This article has thus reviewed mainstream macroeconomics, PKE, comparative political economy, and Marxist political economy. For each of these we find some insight, but the balance between theoretical advances and empirical advances is uneven. Mainstream economics, because of its rationality and market clearing assumptions, has a limited ability to conceptually understand the dynamics emanating from real estate markets. Still it has provided a substantial amount of the empirical research on wealth effects and, more recently, evidence on financial cycles. PKE is much better positioned to analyze housing finance, as it has endogenous money creation and financial instability at its core, but it has been slow to provide empirical applications. Political economy approaches have also proceeded unevenly. Like mainstream economics, the VoC approach is ill-suited to understand the complex dynamics arising from housing, because of its focus on supply-side factors and competitiveness. However, other parts of comparative political economy have advanced research on housing, inspired by the financialization literature and PK analysis of growth models. It has also, with a heavy dose of institutionalism and economic history, motivated a comparative research on mortgage finance systems. Marxist political economy highlights rentierism and (intra)class conflict. Using asset and wealth surveys in a class-relational approach can be a useful starting point in tracing power relations and the pervasiveness of antagonistic (intra)class interests. For the United Kingdom, for instance, some 6 percent of households derive on average as much as one-fifth of their total annual income from rental payments. However, the challenge lies, first, in defining theoretically grounded delineations when class boundaries are themselves unsettled and, second, in taking the class-relational approach to housing forward empirically—in particular, linking potential housing-related class fragmentation to capital–labor relations as well as macroeconomic aggregates.

In short, an adequate macroeconomics and political economy of housing remains to be developed. It will have to build on PK macroeconomic theory to understand the debt dynamics emanating from the housing sector but also incorporate mainstream quantitative methods. Its impact is large, both on macroeconomic dynamics, where it has powerful influence on investment and consumption, and on financial stability, as mortgage debt constitutes most of household debt and an increasing share of bank balance sheets. House price dynamics tend to have a positive feedback on credit (as housing is used as collateral) and thus are prone to speculative bubbles. Housing has a powerful impact on political dynamics in that it can shape identities and political preferences, political economy approaches finding negative correlations between homeownership and support for redistribution and social insurance as well as new housing development. It raises interesting questions for class analysis, as parts of the working class do own their homes (often, they also owe a lot of mortgage debt), which can affect their social identify as well as their political orientation.

Notes

1. There were 111 cases in which the primary residence was rented but rental income derived. Eighty-two of these rental incomes derive from BTL or land overseas or other property, and they were classified as rentiers. The remaining 29 cases did not own property of any sort or have mortgages, some even deriving benefits. Their rental income might derive from peer-to-peer renting schemes. They were classified as renters.
2. For this we base our calculations on the UK Living Costs and Food Survey, 2016–2017 (Department for Environment, Food, and Office for National Statistics 2018). See Table A3 for distribution by tenure.

References

Aalbers, Manuel B., and Brett Christophers. 2014a. "Centring Housing in Political Economy." *Housing, Theory and Society* 31 (4):373–94. doi: 10.1080/14036096.2014.947082.

Aalbers, Manuel B., and Brett Christophers. 2014b. "The Housing Question under Capitalist Political Economies." *Housing, Theory and Society* 31 (4):422–8. doi: 10.1080/14036096.2014.947083.

Aikman, David, Andrew G. Haldane, and Benjamin D. Nelson. 2015. "Curbing the Credit Cycle." *The Economic Journal* 125 (585):1072–109. doi: 10.1111/ecoj.12113.

Aizenman, Joshua, and Yothin Jinjarak. 2014. "Real Estate Valuation, Current account and Credit Growth Patterns, before and after the 2008–9 Crisis." *Journal of International Money and Finance* 48 (November):249–70. doi: 10.1016/j.jimonfin.2014.05.016.

Ansell, Ben. 2014. "The Political Economy of Ownership: Housing Markets and the Welfare State." *American Political Science Review* 108 (2):383–402. doi: 10.1017/S0003055414000045.

Arcand, Jean Louis, Enrico Berkes, and Ugo Panizza. 2015. "Too Much Finance?" *Journal of Economic Growth* 20 (2):105–48. doi: 10.1007/s10887-015-9115-2.

Arestis, Philip, and Ana Rosa González. 2014. "Bank Credit and the Housing Market in OECD Countries." *Journal of Post Keynesian Economics* 36 (3):467–90. doi: 10.2753/PKE0160-3477360304.

Arrighi, Giovanni. 1994. *The Long Twentieth Century*. London, UK: Verso.

Arundel, Rowan. 2017. "Equity Inequity: Housing Wealth Inequality, Inter and Intra-Generational Divergences, and the Rise of Private Landlordism." *Housing, Theory and Society* 34 (2):176–200. doi: 10.1080/14036096.2017.1284154.

Badarinza, Cristian, and Tarun Ramadorai. 2018. "Home Away from Home? Foreign Demand and London House Prices." *Journal of Financial Economics* 130 (3):532–55. doi: 10.1016/j.jfineco.2018.07.010.

Barrell, Ray, E. Philip Davis, Dilruba Karim, and Iana Liadze. 2010. "Bank Regulation, Property Prices and Early Warning Systems for Banking Crises in OECD Countries." *Journal of Banking and Finance* 34 (9):2255–64. doi: 10.1016/j.jbankfin.2010.02.015.

Basu, Deepankar. 2018. "Marx's Analysis of Ground-Rent: Theory, Examples and Applications." UMass Amherst Economics Department Working Papers No 241. University of Massachusetts Amherst, Department of Economics. Amherst, MA (USA).

Bernanke, Ben S., Mark, Gertler, and Simon Gilchrist. 1999. "The Financial Accelerator in a Quantitative Business Cycle Framework." In *Handbook of Macroeconomics*, edited by John B. Taylor and Michael Assous, 1341–92. North-Holland, Netherlands: Elsevier.

Berry, Michael. 1986. "Housing Provision and Class Relations under Capitalism: Some Implications of Recent Marxist Class Analysis." *Housing Studies* 1 (2):109–21. doi: 10.1080/02673038608720568.

Berry, Michael. 2014. "Housing Provision and Class Relations under Capitalism: Comment on Christophers and Aalbers." *Housing, Theory and Society* 31 (4):395–403. doi: 10.1080/14036096.2014.947079.

Bezemer, Dirk. 2014. "Schumpeter Might Be Right Again: The Functional Differentiation of Credit." *Journal of Evolutionary Economics* 24 (5):935–50. doi: 10.1007/s00191-014-0376-2.

Bezemer, Dirk, Maria Grydaki, and Lu Zhang. 2016. "More Mortgages, Lower Growth?" *Economic Inquiry* 54 (1):652–74. doi: 10.1111/ecin.12254.

Blackwell, Timothy, and Sebastian Kohl. 2018. "The Origins of National Housing Finance Systems: A Comparative Investigation into Historical Variations in Mortgage Finance Regimes." *Review of International Political Economy* 25 (1):49–74. doi: 10.1080/09692290.2017.1403358.

Bofinger, Peter, Sebastian Debes, Johannes Gareis, and Eric Mayer. 2013. "Monetary Policy Transmission in a Model with Animal Spirits and House Price Booms and Busts." *Journal of Economic Dynamics and Control* 37 (12):2862–81. doi: 10.1016/j.jedc.2013.08.002.

Boone, Lawrence, Claude, Giorno, and Pete Richardson. 1998. "Stock Market Fluctuations and Consumption Behaviour: Some Recent Evidence." OECD Economics Department Working Papers 208. Paris, France: Organisation for Economic Cooperation and Development.

Borio, Claudio. 2012. "The Financial Cycle and Macroeconomics: What Have We Learnt". BIS Working Papers 395. Basel, Switzerland: Bank of International Settlement.

Buiter, Willem H. 2010. "Housing Wealth Isn't Wealth." *Economics: The Open-Access, Open-Assessment E-Journal* 4 (2010-22):1. doi: 10.5018/economics-ejournal.ja.2010-22.

Case, Karl, Robert Shiller, and John Quigley. 2005. "Comparing Wealth Effects: The Stock Market versus the Housing Market." *Advances in Macroeconomics* 5 (1):1235.

Christophers, Brett. 2018. *The New Enclosure - The Appropriation of Public Land in Neoliberal Britain.* London, UK; New York, NY: Verso.

Clift, Ben. 2014. *Comparative Political Economy - States, Markets and Global Capitalism.* Basingstoke (UK): Macmillan International Higher Education.

Coelho, Miguel, Sebastian Dellepiane-Avellaneda, and Vigyan Ratnoo. 2017. "The Political Economy of Housing in England." *New Political Economy* 22 (1):31–60. doi: 10.1080/ 13563467.2016.1195346.

Crouch, Colin. 2009. "Privatised Keynesianism: An Unacknowledged Policy Regime." *The British Journal of Politics and International Relations* 11 (3):382–99. doi: 10.1111/j.1467-856X.2009.00377.x.

De Grauwe, Paul. 2012. "Booms and Busts in Economic Activity: A Behavioral Explanation." *Journal of Economic Behavior and Organization* 83 (3):484–501. doi: 10.1016/j.jebo.2012.02.013.

Department For Environment, Food, and Office For National Statistics. 2018. "Living Costs and Food Survey, 2016–2017". UK Data Service. https://beta.ukdataservice.ac.uk/datacatalogue/doi/?id=8351#1.

Dieci, Roberto, and Frank Westerhoff. 2012. "A Simple Model of a Speculative Housing Market." *Journal of Evolutionary Economics* 22 (2):303–29. doi: 10.1007/s00191-011-0259-8.

Drehman, Mathias, Claudio, Borio, and Kostas Tsatsaronis. 2012. "Characterising the Financial Cycle: Don't Lose Sight of the Medium Term!" BIS Working Papers 380. Basel, Switzerland: Bank of International Settlement.

Dutt, Amitava Krishna. 2006. "Maturity, Stagnation and Consumer Debt: A Steindlian Approach." *Metroeconomica* 57 (3):339–64. doi: 10.1111/j.1467-999X.2006.00246.x.

Edel, Matthew. 1982. "Home Ownership and Working Class Unity." *International Journal of Urban and Regional Research* 6 (2):205–22. doi: 10.1111/j.1468-2427.1982.tb00574.x.

Eggertsson, Gauti B., and Paul Krugman. 2012. "Debt, Deleveraging, and the Liquidity Trap: A Fisher-Minsky-Koo Approach*." *The Quarterly Journal of Economics* 127 (3): 1469–1513. doi: 10.1093/qje/qjs023.

Erturk, Ismail, and Stefano Solari. 2007. "Banks as Continuous Reinvention." *New Political Economy* 12 (3):369–88. doi: 10.1080/13563460701485599.

Fallis, George. 1985. *Housing Economics.* Toronto, Canada and Vancouver, Canada: Butterworth & Co.

Fernandez, Rodrigo, and Manuel B. Aalbers. 2017. "Housing and Capital in the Twenty-First Century: Realigning Housing Studies and Political Economy." *Housing, Theory and Society* 34 (2):151–58. doi: 10.1080/14036096.2017.1293379.

Fessler, Pirmin, and Martin Schürz. 2018. *The Functions of Wealth: Renters, Owners and Capitalists across Europe and the United States. WP Österreichisch Nationalbank 223.* Vienna, Austria: Österreichische Nationalbank.

Glaeser, Edward L. 2013. "A Nation of Gamblers: Real Estate Speculation and American History." *American Economic Review: Papers and Proceedings* 103 (3):1–42. doi: 10.1257/aer.103.3.1.

Godley, Wynne. 1999. "Seven Unsustainable Processes." Levy Institute Special Report. New York, NY: Levy Institute. http://www.levyinstitute.org/pubs/sevenproc.pdf.

Godley, Wynne, and Marc Lavoie. 2007. *Monetary Economics*. New York, UK: Palgrave Macmillan.

Goodhart, C., and B. Hofmann. 2008. "House Prices, Money, Credit, and the Macroeconomy." *Oxford Review of Economic Policy* 24 (1):180–205. doi: 10.1093/oxrep/grn009.

Hancock, Lynn, and Gerry Mooney. 2013. "'Welfare Ghettos' and the 'Broken Society': Territorial Stigmatization in the Contemporary UK." *Housing, Theory and Society* 30 (1): 46–64. doi: 10.1080/14036096.2012.683294.

Harvey, David. 1974. "Class-Monopoly Rent, Finance Capital and the Urban Revolution." *Regional Studies* 8 (3–4):239–55. doi: 10.1080/09595237400185251.

Harvey, David. 1982. 'Labor, Capital, and Class Struggle around the Built Environment in Advanced Capitalist Societies'. In *Classes, Power, and Conflict*, edited by Anthony Giddens and David Held, 545–61. London, UK and Basingstoke, UK: Macmillan.

Hasan, Mohammad S., and Majid Taghavi. 2002. "Residential Investment, Macroeconomic Activity and Financial Deregulation in the UK: An Empirical Investigation." *Journal of Economics and Business* 54 (4):447–62. doi: 10.1016/S0148-6195(02)00093-0.

IMF. 2000. 'Asset Prices and the Business Cycle'. Chapter 3 of World Economic Outlook. Washington, DC: International Monetary Fund.

Jordà, Òscar, Moritz Schularick, and Alan M. Taylor. 2016. "The Great Mortgaging: Housing Finance, Crises and Business Cycles." *Economic Policy* 31 (85):107–52. doi: 10.1093/epolic/eiv017.

Kapeller, Jakob, and Bernhard Schütz. 2014. "Debt, Boom, Bust: A Theory of Minsky-Veblen Cycles." *Journal of Post Keynesian Economics* 36 (4):781–814. doi: 10.2753/PKE0160-3477360409.

Kemp, Peter A. 2015. "Private Renting after the Global Financial Crisis." *Housing Studies* 30 (4):601–20. doi: 10.1080/02673037.2015.1027671.

Kim, Yun K., Gilberto, Tadeu Lima, and Mark Setterfield. 2017. "Political Aspects of Household Debt." Working Papers 1724. New School for Social Research, Department of Economics.

Kindleberger, Charles P. 1993. *A Financial History of Western Europe*. 2nd ed. Oxford, UK: Oxford University Press.

Knoll, Katharina, Moritz Schularick, and Thomas Steger. 2017. "No Price like Home: Global House Prices, 1870–." *American Economic Review* 107 (2):331–53. doi: 10.1257/aer.20150501.

Kohl, Sebastian. 2018. "More Mortgages, More Homes? the Effect of Housing Financialization on Homeownership in Historical Perspective." *Politics and Society* 46 (2):177–203. doi: 10.1177/0032329218755750.

Langley, Paul. 2007. "Uncertain Subjects of Anglo-American Financialization." *Cultural Critique* 65 (1):67–91. doi: 10.1353/cul.2007.0009.

Lavoie, Marc., and Engelbert Stockhammer. 2013. *Wage-Led Growth. An Equitable Strategy for Economic Recovery*. London, UK: Palgrave MacMillan.

Levine, Ross. 1997. "Financial Development and Economic Growth: Views and Agenda." *Journal of Economic Literature* 35 (2):688–726.

Maki, Dean M., and Michael G. Palumbo. 2001. "Disentangling the Wealth Effect: A Cohort Analysis of Household Saving in the 1990s." Finance and Economics Discussion Series 2001-21. Board of Governors of the Federal Reserve System.

Mian, Atif, Kamalesh Rao, and Amir Sufi. 2013. "Household Balance Sheets, Consumption, and the Economic Slump*." *The Quarterly Journal of Economics* 128 (4):1687–1726. doi: 10.1093/qje/qjt020.

Mian, Atif, and Amir Sufi. 2018. "Finance and Business Cycles: The Credit-Driven Household Demand Channel." *Journal of Economic Perspectives* 32 (3):31–58. doi: 10.1257/jep.32.3.31.

Minsky, Hyman P. 1978. "The Financial Instability Hypothesis: A Restatement." Paper 180. *Hyman P. Minsky Archive.*

Muellbauer, John. 2007. "Housing, Credit and Consumer Expenditure." Proceedings - Economic Policy Symposium - Jackson Hole. Federal Reserve Bank, Kansas City.

Office For National Statistics, Social Survey Division. 2018. 'Wealth and Assets Survey, Waves 1-5, 2006-2016'. UK Data Service. https://beta.ukdataservice.ac.uk/datacatalogue/doi/?id=7215#7.

Palley, Thomas I. 1994. "Debt, Aggregate Demand, and the Business Cycle: An Analysis in the Spirit of Kaldor and Minsky." *Journal of Post Keynesian Economics* 16 (3):371–90. doi: 10.1080/01603477.1994.11489991.

Park, Joon. 2014. "Land Rent Theory Revisited." *Science and Society* 78 (1):88–109. doi: 10.1521/siso.2014.78.1.88.

Perugini, Cristiano, Jens Hölscher, and Simon Collie. 2016. "Inequality, Credit and Financial Crises." *Cambridge Journal of Economics* 40 (1):227–57. doi: 10.1093/cje/beu075.

Poulantzas, Nicos. 1982. 'On Social Classes'. In *Classes, Power, and Conflict.* edited by Anthony Giddens and David Held, 101–11. London, UK and Basingstoke, UK: Macmillan.

Ryan-Collins, Josh, Toby, Lloyd, and Laurie MacFarlane. 2017. *Rethinking the Economics of Land and Housing.* London, UK: Zed Books.

Ryoo, Soon. 2016. "Household Debt and Housing Bubbles: A Minskian Approach to Boom-Bust Cycles." *Journal of Evolutionary Economics* 26 (5):971–1006. doi: 10.1007/s00191-016-0473-5.

Saunders, Peter. 1984. "Beyond Housing Classes: The Sociological Significance of Private Property Rights in Means of Consumption." *International Journal of Urban and Regional Research* 8 (2):202–27. doi: 10.1111/j.1468-2427.1984.tb00608.x.

Schwartz, Herman, and Leonard Seabrooke. 2008. "Varieties of Residential Capitalism in the International Political Economy: Old Welfare States and the New Politics of Housing." *Comparative European Politics* 6 (3):237–61. doi: 10.1057/cep.2008.10.

Shaikh, Anwar. 2016. *Capitalism Competition, Conflict, Crises.* Oxford, UK: Oxford University Press.

Slacalek, Jiri. 2009. "What Drives Personal Consumption? The Role of Housing and Financial Wealth." *The B.E Journal of Macroeconomics* 9 (1): 1–37. doi: 10.2202/1935-1690.1555.

Soaita, Adriana Mihaela, Beverley Ann Searle, Kim McKee, and Tom Moore. 2017. "Becoming a Landlord: Strategies of Property-Based Welfare in the Private Rental Sector in Great Britain." *Housing Studies* 32 (5):613–37. doi: 10.1080/02673037.2016.1228855.

Stiglitz, Joseph E., and Andrew Weiss. 1981. "Credit Rationing in Markets with Imperfect Information." *The American Economic Review* 71 (3):393–410.

Stockhammer, Engelbert. 2012. "Financialization, Income Distribution and the Crisis." *Investigación Económica* 71 (279):39–70.

Stockhammer, Engelbert, and Rafael Wildauer. 2016. "Debt-Driven Growth? Wealth, Distribution and Demand in OECD Countries." *Cambridge Journal of Economics* 40 (6): 1609–34. doi: 10.1093/cje/bev070.

Watson, Matthew. 2010. "House Price Keynesianism and the Contradictions of the Modern Investor Subject." *Housing Studies* 25 (3):413–26. doi: 10.1080/02673031003711550.

Wood, James D. G. 2018. "The Integrating Role of Private Homeownership and Mortgage Credit in British Neoliberalism." Housing Studies, December, 33 (7):993–1013. doi: 10.1080/02673037.2017.1414159.

Appendix

Table A1. Distribution of profession by tenure type, in percentages.

Profession	Renter	Owner-outright	Owner-mortgage	Rentier
Managerial & prof. occupations	22	44	56	62
Intermediate occupations	18	23	19	24
Routine & manual occupations	50	32	24	13
Never worked/long term unemp.	7	1	0	0
Not classified	3	0	1	1

Note. Calculations based on Wealth and Assets Survey, Wave 5, 2014–2016.

Table A2. Age distribution by tenure type, in percentages.

Age band	Renter	Owner-outright	Owner-mortgage	Rentier
16–24	4	0	0	0
25–34	21	1	18	8
35–44	20	2	30	20
45–54	20	9	32	24
55–64	13	23	14	25
65–74	11	31	3	17
75–84	7	24	1	5
85+	4	9	0	2

Note. Calculations based on Wealth and Assets Survey, Wave 5, 2014–2016.

Table A3. Tenure types, in percentages.

Other	1.2
Owner mortgage	31.2
Owner outright	35.4
Renter-private	16.2
Renter-social	16

Note. Calculations based on U.K, Living Costs and Food Survey, 2016–2017.

Table A4. Net housing costs/ normal weekly disposable income, in percentages.

Decile	Private-renter	Renter-social	Owner-outright	Owner-mortgage
1	57	23	23	80
2	45	17	14	27
3	38	21	13	26
4	30	20	11	18
5	33	22	10	18
6	31	17	9	16
7	27	17	8	14
8	25	13	7	13
9	26	13	6	12
10	24	9	5	13

Note. Calculations based on U.K. Living Costs and Food Survey, 2016–2017.

Marx's Financial Capitalism

Makoto Nishibe

ABSTRACT

This study shows that "financialization," widely accepted as a theoretical framework representing the structural change in modern capitalist economy, is one aspect of the "free investment capitalism" that resulted from globalization and deindustrialization as the long-term institutional and technological trends since the 1970s. Globalization is understood as the tendency for the simultaneous expansion (more accurately, extensive expansion and intensive deepening) of market and the reduction of state and community. Its ultimate goal is free investment capitalism, in which fictitious capital is ubiquitous and free investment in it is totally pursued. The study theoretically sees it as G mode (general mode) capitalist market economy with general commodification of labor power as seen in human capital investment and financialization of labor power.

Financialization and financial capitalism

In recent years, the role of financial markets and the financial industry in economic activities has grown more than that of industrial production, and financial crises have frequently occurred. The structural features of contemporary capitalism became known as financialization in the early 1990s and, in the 21st century, this term became widely shared, from Marxian to post-Keynesian and regulation schools. Despite differences in meaning and emphasis, it is commonly thought that financialization is a theoretical framework representing the structural change in modern capitalist economy. This study, although it shares this problematic setting, is an attempt to look at financialization as one aspect of "free investment capitalism," which resulted from globalization and deindustrialization.

First, I will briefly introduce discussions representative of the Marxian school. According to Lapavitsas, financialization indicates a system transformation of the mature capitalist economy and has three characteristics:

1. independence of monopoly capital from banks and self-finance;
2. expanding financial market intermediaries at banks (investment banking operations) and loans to households and workers; and
3. increase in households' financial debt and financial assets (Lapavitsas 2010).

In addition, Itoh (2010) said that the historical specialty of the subprime crisis is attributable to the increase in workers' assets and liabilities, particularly the "financialization of labor-power" found in the speculative expansion of housing loans and consumer finance related to durable consumer goods, such as automobiles. Both of these authors believed that the characteristics of modern capitalism's financialization lie in the increase of the financial role in households, as well as that of corporations and banks, which is the cause of the subprime crisis.

In note 99, Chapter 3, Volume 1 of *Capital,* Marx (1867), classified monetary crises into two types: the first, which occurred as one phase of every crisis in industry and commerce, and the second, a special type of crisis that originated from "moneyed capital," occurred in banks and exchanges, independently of industry and commerce, and only had reactionary effects on industry and commerce. The first type has occurred in the late boom of industrial cycles in classical capitalism and has been seen before in capitalism. The second type, in modern times, appeared as a monetary and financial instability, such as the collapse of Japan's bubble and the Asian currency crisis in the 1990s.

The first thing to note is that the modern financial crisis represented by the 2008 subprime crisis is closer to the second type than to the first type. Since the 1980s, global excess liquidity was formed by an increase in investment funds by institutional investors, accumulation of internal reserves and self-financing by large enterprises, an increase in household assets and liabilities, an expansion in asset/income disparity, a proliferation of wealthy financial assets, and central banks' monetary easing policies. Large-scale bubbles were intermittently formed by such overaccumulated moneyed capital flowing into real estate, stock, the foreign exchange market, and the financial derivatives market. The collapse of the bubbles caused financial panic, with bank collapses and currency crashes, which led to a crisis involving the collapse of the financial system. Thus, the modern financial crisis was not due to excessive accumulation of industrial capital based on the expansion of traditional bank credit. Fictitious capital markets—such as a derivatives market and a structured commodity market—are formed by the securitization of finance, and a large amount of moneyed capital flowing there forms self-fulfilling bubbles. It creates a systemic risk of a total collapse of the financial system. Therefore, beyond the central bank, public relief by the state or the state coalition (in the case of the European Union) was requested. In this respect, there is a characteristic of monetary crisis in modern financial capitalism.

The next point to remember is that modern finance-led capitalism is different from "finance capital-controlled capitalism"[1] that was dominated by "finance capital" (Hilferding 1910) at the end of the 19th century. In Lenin's (1916) imperialism, it is stated that capital accumulation and concentration has advanced, and when the market shifts from free competition to monopoly, finance capital, as an integrated form of monopoly capital and bank capital, becomes dominant. In contemporary financial capitalism, contrary to the case of finance capital, corporations leave banks, aiming for direct finance and self-finance. On the other hand, banks turn to financial market mediation and household loans. Why did these differences emerge?

Lenin believed that, because the economy of scale works more effectively as heavy chemical industrialization proceeds, the monopoly and oligopoly of industrial capital progresses so that production is socialized. Hence, if "bookkeeping and control" were extended to all areas of production and distribution, it would be possible to abolish commerce and money and to operate the economy of a country like a large factory, through quantity planning. He conceived a centralized planned economy based on the "one country as one factory" theory and led the Russian Revolution. Whether the Soviet-type socialist economy is viable was discussed in the socialist economic calculation debate. Hayek (1948) criticized the centralized planning of a socialist economy because there are fundamental defects that only the market can overcome, such as the difficulty in collection, discovery, and creation of knowledge.[2] Nevertheless, until the first half of the 20th century, production technology remained heavy and large, and industrial structure was monopolized, so the defect of Lenin's vision was not revealed and the Soviet-type socialism managed to survive.

However, as deindustrialization rapidly proceeded in developed countries in the 1970s, production technology transformed into light and small, and industrial structure became more oligopolistic or monopolistically competitive. Nonprice competition, such as product differentiation among oligopolistic suppliers, intensified. Consumers placed more importance on quality than on quantity, on service or information than on material goods, and on design rather than on function. Then, as both process and product innovations in information and communication technology (ICT) industries rapidly progressed, the problem of centralized planning—as a difficulty in gathering, discovering, and creating knowledge—gradually became more serious. Lenin's vision, thus, gradually lost its validity, and this ultimately resulted in the collapse of Soviet-type socialism. Although the Keynesian welfare state, which maintained macro-economic financial and fiscal policies after the 1970s, also deepened the confusion, financial capitalism emerged.

Rearranging the history of the 20th century as above, we can now understand that the objective grounds for the expansion of neoliberalism and the collapse of the socialist countries lay in a shift toward deindustrialization in production technology and industrial structure. The combination of the financial big bang that globalization caused in the financial world and the financial innovation that advanced on the basis of the ICT revolution resulted in the financialization of the economy, industry, households, and motivation. Under the long-term tendency for a change toward globalization, shifts in production technology and industrial structure through deindustrialization resulted in financialization.

Globalization in the depths of financialization and free investment capitalism as its ultimate goal

What, then, is the globalization that lies in the depths of financialization? Globalization is often understood as institutional and policy changes, such as liberalization and deregulation, caused by a thought or an ideology called neoliberalism. However, it is rather the consequence of objective economic tendencies, such as deindustrialization. Globalization apparently can be recognized as a trend toward a global single free market accompanied by development of transportation technology as well as ICT and financial expansion. However, a more abstract and theoretical definition is necessary.

Polanyi (1944) depicted market (money exchange, private, freedom, and blue), state (redistribution, public, equality, and white), and community (reciprocity, common, fraternity, and red) as the integrative principles enabling the reproduction of socio-economy. My interpretation here is that blue, white, and red as tricolor of French national flag represent three political ideas of the French Revolution—freedom, equality, and fraternity—which respectively correspond to economic adjustment principles: money exchange in market, redistribution in state, and reciprocity in community. By using these three integrative principles, globalization is more deeply understood as the tendency for the expansion of market and the reduction of state and community to progress simultaneously, and the process in which the private and individual areas become relatively larger than the public and common areas. In view of political thought, it represents the growth of freedom (blue) and the decline of equality (white) and fraternity (red; see Figure 1).

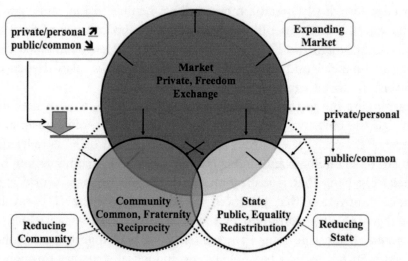

Figure 1. Globalization.

Here, let me make two definitions:

1. "Extensive expansion of the market" is expanding the market size of existing products and extending the geographical region of the market.
2. "Intensive deepening of the market" is the conversion of public or common free goods into private paid goods as commodity (commodification), or the innovation and sale of new products (new commodification) through a shift of the integrative principles from state (redistribution) and community (reciprocity) to market (monetary exchange).

Then, we can see that globalization is the rapidly progressing tendency of both the extensive expansion of the market and the intensive deepening of the market in modern capitalism.

Market, here, is a decentralized market as a chain network of bilateral money buying and selling, not a centralized market as an auctioneer type of price mechanism only with *numéraire,* as in neoclassical economics. In the decentralized market, two kinds of freedom are distinguished. The first is freedom of trade—that is, consumers can use money to buy and sell various kinds of goods (use value) without any restriction. The second is freedom of investment—that is, investors can use money to buy and sell various capital (revenue opportunities) without any restriction. Both are "negative liberties," but the latter is a higher-order freedom that presupposes the former. Although trade has the ultimate goal of the consumption of use value or enjoyment of utility, investment seeks an abstract and endless purpose for profit.[3]

Globalization is ultimately oriented toward free investment capitalism and has the following aspects: When an individual invests in fictitious capital—called human capital—all goods and services, including labor power, become capitalistic (produced) products for profit (universalization of capitalist products). In addition, companies employ labor power as fictitious capital to innovate, produce, and sell not only industrial products but also financial products, such as stocks and bonds, and acquire founder's profit (universalization of fictitious capital). As a result, people, goods, and money move globally in search of high profitability (universalization of investment), as investment is selected based on the rate of return.

In Chapter 29, Volume 3, of *Capital*, Marx (1894), called "real capital," on the one hand, the capital of real entities, such as physical means of production, including machines, factories, and laborers, which usefully function in production. On the other hand, he called fictitious capital the stocks and bonds, which are "nothing but accumulated claims, or legal titles, to future production." In this chapter, he indicated that the price of "bonds (the state's promissory note)" as fictitious capital can be obtained by capitalization—that is, by calculating the sum of the streams of the discounted present value of expected future profit. In case of a consol, which is a perpetual bond with a certain amount of coupon, say, c, its price, p, by capitalization at a current rate of interest, i, is simply calculated as $p = c/i$.

Hilferding (1910) claimed that as the stock and bond markets dealing in such fictitious capital spread, the dividends received by the shareholders would approach interest, and the capital with profit and the capital with interest would eventually become equivalent. Therefore, the founder would obtain the founder's profit, calculated by capitalizing the expected profit for the capital invested at the time of the establishment of the company. For example, if the founding capital is K and the expected profit rate is r^e, the security price of all shares that capitalize the expected profit of the following term Kr^e with a market interest rate i is calculated as Kr^e/i, and, if $r^e > i$, the founder's profit $R = K(r^e/i - 1)$ is positive.

Fictitious capital is a bundle of various claims, not just the bonds and stocks of modern times. Futures, options, and swaps, which are derivative instruments, are all digitized and can be traded by people or AI robots on the internet. In the case of options, we conduct investment by buying and selling market priced packages consisting of the rights to buy (call) and the rights to sell (put) on a base asset (a certain stock, bond, stock price index, etc.) by a certain time (the expiration date) for a certain price (the strike price). Collateralized debt obligations and credit default swaps, which became famous in the subprime crisis, are also fictitious capital. The former is a type of structured asset-backed security (ABS) issued as collateral with mortgages, loans, and bonds (both public and corporate bonds). Its composition is flexible, as there are diverse assets for its structure, from "low risk and low return" to "high risk and high return." With the development of ICT, such ABSs for liquidating and off-balancing can be easily and massively produced and sold to investors around the world. The ultimate goal of globalization is idealized as free investment capitalism—that is, a world in which such fictitious capital is ubiquitous.

In free investment capitalism, labor power is also converted into fictitious capital, called human capital. Here, let us examine fictitious capital in education and training. As Becker's (1964) human capital theory explained, fictitious capital in education is realized if students invest monetary expenses (such as tuition and interest on education loans) and opportunity costs (such as time of education and training) to acquire professional knowledge and skills to increase the expected earnings they can see in the future. Acquisition of qualifications and skills through a professional education and vocational training of workers is also considered to be human capital formation. The present value of human capital is the sum of a stream of present value obtained by discounting the expected increase of income at a constant interest rate. For example, suppose you expect to work for 40 years after you graduate from university. The expected returns (the difference in salary between university graduates and high school graduates) are 1 million yen each year, and the discount rate is 1 percent. Then, the present value (discounted present value; DPV) of human capital through university education can be calculated as follows:

$$\text{DPV} = \sum_{i=1}^{40} \frac{1,000,000}{(1+0.01)^i} = 32,830,000 \text{ Yen.}$$

Human capital investment is feasible if current education costs fall below this amount. Once the method of capitalization is applied to education and training, human beings are regarded as a stock of human capital that produces future income flows, so fictitious capital in education and training is established. If we extend this investors' logic to marriage choices and household chores, childcare, and nursing care of family members, fictitious capital can be found everywhere in one's personal life. Financialization of workers through households' increased financial assets and liabilities represents a situation in which workers or their agents (institutional investors who operate funds and insurance) have been investing, based on projected future returns (income and capital gains), rather than saving money in deposits with a given interest. Their investment is in larger quantities of many types of fictitious capital, such as volatile and risky real estate, stocks and bonds, derivatives (including FX and futures), and even human capital. This omnipresence of the replicator called fictitious capital is, thus, the most important characteristic of free investment capitalism, which is the ultimate goal of globalization.

Free investment capitalism differs from the "self-regulating market" referred to by Polanyi (1944) in *The Great Transformation*. In the end of the 18th century, labor, land, and money became fictitious commodities that were objects for money exchange, and the self-regulating market was established in the industrial capitalism of the 19th century ("external commodification of labor power"). After the 1970s, when labor power, next to land and money, had become a "capitalist product"—that is, a general commodity sold for profit purposes (hereafter, "general commodification of labor power")—fictitious capital was extended to include labor power. Therefore, the leading characteristic of modern free investment capitalism is Marx's fictitious capital instead of Polanyi's "fictitious commodities." In free investment capitalism, all services and rights—including labor power, which used to be regarded as a simple commodity—are sold as "revenue opportunities" or fictitious capital. Globalization has serious negative impacts not only on the economy but also on society, culture, and ethics.

The contemporary problems of globalization have spread into economic ones, such as the financial instability found in the repetition of bubble expansion and collapse, increase in unemployment and nonregular employment, economic inequality, and expansion of poverty. However, they have also spread into social and cultural ones, such as the weakening of people's connections; the collapse of communities such as families, schools, and neighborhoods; loss of diversity; and moral decay. The root cause can be found in the fact that the transformation from fictitious commodities into fictitious capital was caused by extensive expansion and intensive deepening of the market, which severely damaged community (reciprocity) and state (redistribution).

Three modes of 'internalization of the market' and evolution of the capitalist economy

"Internalization of the market" is the logic for the establishment and evolution of capitalism. Marx explained this in *A Contribution to the Critique of Political Economy* (1859) and in Chapter 2, in *Capital* (1867), as follows:

> In fact, the exchange of commodities evolves originally not within primitive communities, but on their margins, on their borders, the few points where they come into contact with other communities. This is where barter begins and moves thence into the interior of the community, exerting a disintegrating influence upon it. (Marx 1859: S.35–36)

> The exchange of commodities begins where communities have their boundaries, at their points of contact with other communities, or with members of the latter.

Table 1. Three modes of commodification in internalization of the market.

	Modes of commodification	Place of commodification	Purpose of production	Frequency of monetary exchange	Degree of economic integration by Market
I	External commodification	Outside of community and state	Consumption	Casual	Low
II	Internal commodification	Inside community and state	Income	Frequent	Medium
III	General commodification	Disappearance of community and state	Profit	Constant	High

> However, as soon as products have become commodities in the external relations of a community, they also, by reaction, become commodities in the internal life of the communities. (Marx 1867: S.102–103)

Markets formed as a chain of commodity exchanges emerged and expanded outside communities and states (on their borders), penetrated to their interior, disassembled redistribution and reciprocity as the internal socioeconomic principles, and replaced them with money exchanges in the market. As a result, goods become commodities, even inside communities and states.[4] Although I include state, which was not mentioned in Marx's quotes, such a theory of internalization of the market should become an important "leading thread" for economics.[5]

The pattern that markets arising between communities and states prevent reproduction of the substantive economy and reorganize it based on the exchange relationship forms the evolutionary process through which the capitalist economy emerged through the generation and development of the market economy. To clarify the logic of this intensive deepening of markets, I call the process "internalization of the market," in which capital, as a circular form of the market derived from the commodity relationship, permeates and dissolves the nonmarket society and self-organizes the economy again.

There are three modes of internalization of the market: external commodification, internal commodification, and general commodification (Table 1). As commodification progresses asI→II→III, the degree of integration in which the market dominates the real economy increases. This is merely a typical pattern, and in actual history, a sequence involving bypassing modes and retrograding may occur. The capitalist market economy is a market economy in which general goods other than labor power and land are all produced and sold for the purpose of profit, on the premise of the labor market's existence. It is a special market economy, derived by combining two commodifications related to general goods and labor power (Table 2). Accordingly, "economy includes market economy, which, in turn, includes capitalist (market) economy" holds.

Table 2. Evolution of capitalist economy through shifts in the modes of commodification of labor power.

I.	External commodification of general goods
II.	Internal commodification of general goods
III.	General commodification of general goods
IV.	General commodification of general goods + External commodification of labor power = Establishment of capitalist market economy
	1. Capitalist market economy with external commodification of labor power (E Mode)
	2. Capitalist market economy with internal commodification of labor power (I Mode)
	3. Capitalist market economy with general commodification of labor power (G Mode)

A capitalist economy will evolve as the intensive deepening of market progresses and the mode of commodification of labor power shifts to external commodification, internal commodification, and general commodification. In the past, labor power was produced in-house in the community as a family and was a "simple commodity" that did not produce profit (E mode). When housework and childcare were indispensable for reproducing the labor power in the family community, they were naturally regarded as free-of-charge activities, "shadow work," which did not involve money (Illich 1981). However, domestic labor has gradually been recognized as representing the opportunity costs associated with the loss of income opportunities in the market, and it became explicitly added as the cost of labor reproduction (I mode). Furthermore, as seen in human capital investment and financialization of labor power, labor power also became a capitalist commodity or fictitious capital pursuing profit (G mode). As a result of this type of globalization, the reciprocity and redistribution principles were replaced with a monetary market relationship and, seemingly, family as the last community has been transformed into an industrial sector that supplies labor power commodity capitalistically.

In the evolution process of capitalism through a mode change of the commodification of labor power, what is the average profit rate for capitalists and the real wage rate for workers—that is, how does the distribution relation changes between labor and management, and what does innovation mean in general commodification of labor power?[6]

In E mode, labor power is disadvantageously evaluated compared to general commodities because domestic labor costs and profits are not included in labor power, but domestic labor costs are incurred in I mode. Furthermore, in G mode, in which labor power demands the same profit rate as that of general commodities, labor power is evaluated as equal to general commodities, so that the status of workers and living standards both increase. The mode of commodification of labor power changes in E, I, and G and, as a result of the inequality between general commodities and labor power in price determination disappearing, the real wage rate rises and the profit rate decreases. This can be called the law of tendency for a decline in the rate of profit with internalization of the market. In G mode, income distribution is advantageous to the labor side, but as it is determined endogenously at the same time as the relative price, the requirement for a rise in the money wage rate by the trade union will only result in a price increase that is proportional to it.[7]

In E mode and I mode, innovation only benefits capitalists. However, in G mode, technological innovation that reduces the cost of general commodities raises the real wage rate and profit rate, and technological innovation that lowers labor cost decreases the real wage rate and raises the profit rate. Innovation that incentivizes both laborers and capitalists now progresses at an accelerated pace, and superprofits continue to be dynamically created. Thus, the capitalist economy itself finds solutions to the problem of the profit rate decrease by changing the mode of labor commodification, and it evolves to create further potentiality.

If capitalism seeks profits for its growth not from exploitation of surplus labor in production but from temporary quasi-rents through innovation, the information and service industries, in which it is relatively easy to create a "difference" through innovation, must largely grow. As a result, deindustrialization accelerates, and fictitious capitalization progresses further. In capitalism, financialization of labor power represents a dilution of the class relationship between capital and labor. Although workers remain wage earners and consumers, they are also approaching capitalists or investors as owners of tangible and intangible assets (real estate, financial products, and human capital), including moneyed capital (fictitious capital). In such a world, the profits earned through trading commodities are created more from innovation activities of services and information involving finance than from production activities of physical goods. Even automobile production activities can be regarded only as activities replicating design information on technique, function, and lifestyle in materials.

Globalization is a process that expands its potential by introducing mutations in parts of capitalist replicators so that capitalism can evolve autonomously to free investment capitalism. Marx said in *Capital* that "individuals (capitalists and land owners) are dealt with here only in so far as they are the personifications of economic categories, the bearers of particular class-relations and interests" (1867), and he virtually admitted that capital was a social "replicator" (meme) and human beings were only a "vehicle" operated by it. The globalization of modern capitalism attempts to build up all subjects as investors. "All people should become free investors" is its slogan. Its limit is pure capitalism, in which fictitious capital is ubiquitous—that is, free investment capitalism, in which financialization of labor power is expanding. However, there is an increasing disparity between these trends of contemporary capitalism and the conditions in which human beings live their daily lives.

Notes

1. In Germany and Japan, finance capital was actually dominant and, although Hilferding never called it so, it can be named as such.
2. See Nishibe (1996) regarding the contents of the socialist economic calculation debate—in particular, the parallelism in Hayek's criticism of socialist planning and his criticism of the general equilibrium theory and its related knowledge problems.
3. Investment also implies self-directed involvement in choosing clothes and acquiring them by themselves, and freedom of investment can also be directed toward "positive freedom." This may suggest one to consider beyond capitalism and globalization.
4. Although "state" does not appear in the related text by Marx, I added it in the sense according to the views of K. Polanyi.
5. Kozo Uno (1980, 2016) focused on this discussion. He argued, in the beginning of the principle of political economy, the theory of circulation—that is, that various forms of circulation (the market formers) of commodities, money, and capital emerge successively outside social reproduction and penetrate the community. He could, thus, explain the "extrinsic" character of forms of circulation such as commodities, money, and capital, without addressing labor value and the reproduction of the real economy.
6. Here, I present no model analysis for these problems, so I will introduce only the results. Readers interested in the analysis should refer to Nishibe (2015).
7. Here, when the mode of commodification of labor power advances as E→I→G and shifts to G mode representing the labor power's fictitious capitalization, it can be described as fully developed investment capitalism, but it is just a simplification. In investment capitalism, it is extremely emphasized that workers with special skills and licenses—such as lawyers and doctors, as well as college students and craftsmen—can be said to be owners of fictitious capital if university education and skill training are regarded as an accumulation of human capital. In reality, it should be seen that the G mode and previous modes are mixed. For example, although the creative class with professional skills reaches the G mode, workers doing simple labor that does not require as much skill and expertise remain in the E mode, forming the group of nonregular workers and industrial reserve army. In this case, class differentiation occurs (Nishibe 2015).

References

Becker, Gary. 1964. *Human Capital: A Theoretical and Empirical Analysis, with Special Reference to Education*. Chicago: University of Chicago Press.

Hayek, Friedrich. 1948. *Individualism and Economic Order*. London: Routledge.

Hilferding, Rudolf. 1910. *Das Finanzkapital. Eine Studie Über Die Jüngste Entwicklung Des Kapitalismus*. Vienna, Austria: Wiener Volksbuchhandlung.

Illich, Ivan. 1981. *Shadow Work*. Salem, New Hampshire and London: Marion Boyars.

Itoh, Makoto. 2010. "From Subprime to the Great Depression." *Political Economy Quarterly (Kikan Keizai Riron)* 47(1):4–14.

Lapavitsas, Costas. 2010. "Financialization and Capitalist Accumulation: Structural Accounts of the Crisis of 2007–9." *Political Economy Quarterly (Kikan Keizai Riron)* 47(1):42-55 (Translated by Masao Yokouchi).

Lenin, Vladimir. 1916. *Imperialism, the Highest Stage of Capitalism*. Collected Works. Vol. 22, Moscow, Russia: Progress Publishers.

Marx, Karl. 1859. *A Contribution to the Critique of Political Economy*. Moscow, Russia: Progress Publishers.

Marx, Karl. 1867. 1894. *Capital*. Vol. I, III. Moscow: Progress Publishers.

Nishibe, Makoto. 1996. *Genealogy of Market Images: Visions over Economic Calculation Debate* as *Shijyozo no Keifugaku: Keizai Keisan Ronso wo meguru Vijyon*. Tokyo: Toyo Keizai Shinpo Sha.

Nishibe, Makoto. 2015. "Globalization: Evolution of Capitalist Market Economy through 'Internalization of the Market." *Evolutionary and Institutional Economics Review* 12(1): 31–60. Springer. doi: 10.1007/s40844-015-0005-2.

Polanyi, Karl. 1944. *The Great Transformation: The Economic and Political Origin of Our Time*. New York: Farrar & Rinehart.

Uno, Kozo. 1980. *Principles of Political Economy. Theory of a Purely Capitalist Society*. Translated from Japanese by Thomas T. Sekine. Brighton, NJ: Atlantic Highlands.

Uno, Kozo. 2016. *The Types of Economic Policies under Capitalism*. Translated from Japanese by Thomas T. Sekine and edited by John R. Bell. Leiden, Netherlands: Brill.

Financialization and the impasse of capitalism

François Chesnais

ABSTRACT
This article considers the inextricable relationship between globalization and financialization. It then argues that the decisive characteristic of financialization is the preeminence of financial accumulation over productive accumulation and of capital-as-property over capital-as-function. The importance of intercorporate power relationships in the distribution of surplus value is demonstrated. After a short setback in 2009, claims to surplus value have continued to grow faster than its production and appropriation, implying that financial profits have become harder to earn. The outcome is the unabated intensity of asset trading and endemic global financial instability.

Financialization has an inextricable relationship with the globalization and centralization of capital in its three forms and is an all-embracing, many-faceted phenomenon. Behind broad indicators such as the high growth rate of financial assets, notably of government and corporate bonds, including their high proportion relative to domestic and world GDP, the exponential growth of derivatives and the scale of international financial trading, there is a range of important aspects related to the preeminence of the distinctive process of "financial accumulation." This concept was developed by Marx in Part 5 of Volume III of *Capital*[1] in the form of claims on current and future surplus value accompanied by the permeation of "capital-as-function" by "capital-as-property"; by the position of oligopoly and monopsony of highly concentrated industrial and merchant corporations, allowing them to benefit from an "external" appropriation of surplus-value alongside its in-house creation and appropriation; by a radical change in the nature of banking and credit; by the abasement of world money to the point where U.S. bonds represent an escape to safety (De Brunhoff 2004); and by the pervasiveness in contemporary society of the fetishist belief that "money can beget money"(Marx 1981: 516), permitting finance to be "organically embedded in the fabric of social life" (Konings 2010). To these traits must be added a change in the configuration of the dominant class, including its horizon and values, with the emergence of a new breed of political personnel of which Donald Trump is the most aggressive example. This article focuses on the first four processes.

Its starting point is the evidence presented in recent IMF and BIS reports and McKinsey studies concerning the rapid resumption of the growth of world debt following a limited deleveraging after the Great Recession of 2008–2009.[2] The resilience of debt is the result of a process of financial accumulation over 70 or 80 years. The repeated injection of fresh money through quantitative easing by central banks since 2008 has played a role in limiting deleveraging, but the accumulation of interest-bearing loan capital seeking valorization in financial markets has deep institutional foundations that go back to the 1970s. The exponential growth of debt while the world GDP grows at a rate of circa 3.8 percent reflects an overall setting that is completely new in the history of capitalism—namely, the absence of new industries with the capacity to create investment opportunities big enough to launch a new long wave of accumulation (see Gordon 2016; Chesnais 2019). This is not directly attributable to financialization but is aggravated by its traits, which are now deeply marked by the victory of capital-as-property over capital-as-function.

The theory of interest-bearing capital and its accumulation as a distinct process

Interest, wrote Marx, is "nothing but a portion of the profit, *i.e.* of the surplus-value, which the functioning capitalist, whether industrialist or merchant, must pay to the owner and lender of capital in so far as the capital he uses is not his own but borrowed" (Marx 1981: 481). This definition must be extended to dividends paid by contemporary "functioning capitalists" to shareholders who can no longer be characterized as "passive capitalists" but as a group very attentive to the performance of corporate and fund managers while reaping at the same time large sums in the form of interest on government debt.

Marx distinguished between "money-dealing capital" and "money-making" in the form of interest. Banks are engaged in both. Operations requiring a call on "money-dealing capital" are required at the M and M′ moments of the accumulation cycle. For firms they represent costs of circulation. At a given moment in capitalist development, "the division of labor requires that these technical operations, dependent upon the functions of capital, should be performed as far as possible for the capitalist class as a whole by a particular division of agents or capitalists as their exclusive function, these operations being concentrated in their hands." (Marx, 1981: 431)

With the rise of banks, "a part of the industrial capital present in the circulation process separates off and becomes autonomous in the form of money-capital, its capitalist function consisting in that it performs these operations for the entire class of commercial and industrial capitalists" (Marx 1981: 432). Initially this involved only the creation of commercial credit in the form of bills of exchange. With the industrial revolution came the need for investment credit. Banks offered industrial capitalists long-term loans, even if the joint-stock company became the main instrument of productive accumulation by virtue of its capacity to centralize dispersed sums from foreign as well as from domestic sources as well as offering stockholders the privilege of liquidity.

The industrial revolution saw a quantum leap in the appropriation of unpaid labor time and consequently in the mass of money firms kept on their balance sheets to meet the requirement of the circulation process, but also entrusted to their banks sums definable as "latent money capital." If put in a bank, wrote Marx, "this latent money capital may in the interval [before being invested in production; F.C.] exist in the actual shape of 'money that breeds money,' e.g. as interest-bearing deposits in a bank, bills of exchange or securities of one kind or another" (Marx 1978: 164). This led him to reflect in Volume III of *Capital* on the nature of "the accumulation of money capital as such. How far it is, and how far it is *not*, an index of genuine accumulation, i.e., of reproduction on an expanded scale? Is the phenomenon of a 'plethora of capital'—simply a particular expression of industrial overproduction or does it form a separate phenomenon alongside this?" (Marx 1981: 606)

Marx's own reply to these questions was that indeed "the accumulation of capital in the form of loanable money capital can become distinct from and not coincide with actual accumulation, i.e., the expansion of the reproduction process." On account first of the simple reason that "the transformation of money into money capital for loan is a far simpler matter than the transformation of money into productive capital" (Marx 1981: 626), which entails new investment and so depends on the rate of profit and the expansion of markets. In Chapter 31 of Volume III Marx wrote of "the section of profit that is not spent as revenue, being rather designed for accumulation, but which the industrial capitalists concerned do not have any immediate employment for in their own businesses. … Its amount rises with the volume of the capital itself, even given a declining rate of profit. … It constitutes loan capital as a deposit with the banker. Furthermore, loan capital is formed because banks centralize money from other classes. In the case of worker's saving Marx observed that "small amounts, each in themselves incapable of acting in the capacity of money capital, merge together into large masses and thus form a money power" (Marx 1981: 528-529).[3] This holds for "all revenues, in so far as they are only gradually consumed—that is, ground-rent, the higher forms of salary, the incomes of the unproductive classes, etc. All of these assume for a time the form of money revenue and can hence be converted into deposits and thereby into interest-bearing capital (Marx 1981: 634–635).

Concrete drawing rights on surplus-value but fictitious capital

The loan of interest-bearing capital materializes in the form of bonds— namely, drawing rights on previously produced surplus value—appropriated in the case of public bonds indirectly through the levying of taxes and the servicing of government debt. It also materializes in private issues of a part of profit, allowing the characterization to be extended to shares and so to the division between retained profits and dividends. These drawing rights increase the portfolio wealth of those who hold them, who view them as a "capital." But from the standpoint of productive accumulation, they are fictitious capital.

In Marx's words:

> [T]he state has to pay its creditors a certain amount of interest each year for the capital it borrows ... the creditor cannot recall his capital from his debtor, but can only sell his claim, his title of ownership. ... As far as the original creditor A is concerned, the share of annual taxation he receives represents interest on his capital. (1981: 595)

> [In the case of] the stocks of railways, mines, navigation companies (they) represent real capital, i.e. capital invested and functioning in these enterprises as capital. ... But this capital does not exist twice over, once as the capital value of ownership titles (shares) and then again as the capital actually invested, or to be invested, in the enterprises in question. It exists only in the latter form, and a share is nothing but an ownership tittle, *pro rata*, to the surplus-value which this capital is to realize. A may sell this title to B, and B to C. These transactions have no essential effect on the matter. A or B then has transformed his title into capital, but C has transformed his capital into a mere title of ownership to the surplus value expected from this share capital. (Marx 1981: 597).

It is not only individuals who view assets as their "capital." These assets also figure as "capital" on the balance sheets of banks, where they are subject to processes of financial circulation that have no relation to the real economy: "all capital seems to be duplicated, and at some points triplicated, by the various ways in which the same capital, or perhaps even the same claim, appears in different hands in different guises" (Marx 1981: 601).

Contemporary financial accumulation and the issues it raises

At the time Marx wrote, financial accumulation was incipient and largely rhythmed with the economic cycle. With the setting in of the longest basically unbroken period of capitalist expansion from the late 1950s to the mid-1990s, financial accumulation became systemic (Chesnais 2016: 44). The initial impulse given to the large-scale accumulation of interest-bearing capital at the end of the 1960s was the appearance of slowly reinvested profits of U.S. multinational enterprises (MNEs; now known as TNCs) at a time when finance was still closely regulated domestically (e.g., the famous Regulation Q). For this mass of capital to not remain "idle," it was necessary to have the possibility of transforming it into loan capital. This function was performed by London's eurodollar offshore loan capital and money markets. The next step was also initiated by banks located in the city. Following the 1973 jump in oil prices, the step took the form of the recycling of rent from oil (the so-called petrodollars) as syndicated bank loans to developing world governments made at variable rather than fixed interest rates. The ground for the first major large-scale, self-reproducing debt process was thus set. In the wake of financial liberalization by the United States and the jump in U.S. interest rates, the Mexican debt crisis of 1982 marked the start of the Latin American "lost decade" and a reversal of financial flows from South to North. Far from resisting the endogenous process of financial accumulation, governments played a decisive role, from the mid-1960s onward, with a steep push at the turn of 1980s, by adopting measures that dismantled the controls over capital movements (see Helleiner 1994).

At the same time that nonreinvested profits or "corporate hoards" fed financial accumulation, advanced country fiscal deficits became increasingly important. This started with the method introduced in the United States for financing the federal budget through the auction of treasury bonds subsequently negotiated in the secondary financial markets. Investors, notably at that time pension funds and incipient mutual funds became the beneficiaries of massive domestic surplus value through the serving of federal debt. The U.S. example was quickly followed by other OECD countries. Governments could borrow from the wealthy rather than tax them. Whenever GDP growth rates fell below interest rates—as they did significantly from 1992 to 1996 in large parts of the OECD—the cost of the servicing of government debt increased and an ever higher fraction of fiscal revenues had to be earmarked for this purpose.

As trade and investment liberalization progressed—and with it the globalization of the industrial reserve army—global and domestic class relationships shifted in favor of capital, and along with it came changes in income distribution in favor of the upper bracket groups on account of the accumulation of patrimonial (real estate and portfolio) wealth in in the hands of the rich and the very rich. However much these groups might spend,[4] Keynes's theory of the falling propensity of consumption asserted itself, meaning that a part of their income was continually pumped back into financial markets. Since the beginning of the commodities boom in the early 2000s, revenues accumulated by primary producer countries in the form of sovereign wealth funds were used for mergers and acquisitions but also directly invested in the U.S. and British financial markets. The case of oil revenues from the Gulf States, notably when prices soared in 2007–2008, has been documented by Marxist research (Hanieh 2012).

Real and financial accumulation in the 2000s

As the slowing but unbroken period of long-term capital expansion continued, a divergence emerged between the rate of growth of real and of financial accumulation. As estimated by proxies, the size of global financial assets and their pace of growth in comparison to that of world GDP became clearly larger.[5] And so the question arose in the 2000s: Is the accumulation of fictitious capital, of bonds and shares, at a pace higher than GDP growth a cause or a consequence of weak productive investment and public expenditure? The answer would be different for government bonds compared to shares and corporate bonds (a distinction few authors have made). In the first case, as soon as creditors begin to get anxious about their exposure, the mass of drawing rights claimed by, and of surplus value distributed to, bond holders will trigger government austerity policies, thus deferring public investment and hitting workers and pensioners severely (as was notoriously the case in Greece).

In the case of shares, however, one finds diverging accounts of causality. One explanation attributes the diversion of profits by corporations away from productive investment and toward financial markets to the inherent lack of attractiveness of the former. Sweezy (1984) defended this position quite early, relating the reemergence of finance to the return of overall capitalist "stagnation," according to his definition of stagnation.[6] "Capital migrating out of the real economy was happily received in the financial sector. Thus began the process which during the next two decades resulted in the triumph of financial capital" (Sweezy 1984: 47). In a very different analytical framework, the decline of profits retained for investment due to the increase of dividends paid to shareholders and so the fall of productive investment has been quite central to Duménil and Lévy's (2011) critique of "neoliberalism."[7]

Duménil and Lévy's position has been specifically challenged by Williams and Kliman (2014). Their analysis of statistical data up to 2007 led them to the conclusion that firms did not slow down their investments either for lack of funds, which were available on the financial markets, or because of the shift in the distribution of profits between retained profits and dividends, but because the rate of profit fell and so profitable investments declined. The causality is one in which the fall in the rate of profit leads to "forced hoarding" and so to an obligatory turn to valorization on financial markets. The findings of the meticulous work by Krippner (2005) was that the ratio of portfolio income—interest, dividends, and capital-market-investment gains (see Krippner (2005)[8]—to cash flows, which she used as her indicator of financialization, grew from 20 percent in 1980 to 60 percent in 2001. This movement corresponds closely to Kliman's calculation of the movement of the U.S. rate of profit (Kliman 2012). Studies posted recently by Roberts (2018) showed that the first decades of the 21st century saw a further increase in the share of portfolio revenues or "financial profits" in total U.S. corporate profits (Jones 2013). I understand the chain of causality as starting with the fall in the rate of profit in the setting of a technological revolution, which does not possess the necessary features to raise long-term investment, with a capitalist class now deeply marked by the effects of financialization and the victory of capital-as-property over capital-as-function.

Direct confrontation between workers and interest-bearing capital

Interest as a specific form of income is easily identifiable for government debt. With regard to corporations, the situation is more complicated. When large corporations borrow money on the bond markets to increase dividends through share buy-backs, this involves money and asset circulation between these corporations as well as a tight group of funds and banks that manage shares in these corporations. The frontier between interest and dividends becomes vague, if not nonexistent. In his classical commentary Harvey (1982: 257) noted Marx's drift toward a very broad definition of interest:

> Since owners of money are concerned primarily to augment their money by interest, they are presumably indifferent as to whom and for what purposes the money is lent provided the return is secure. This creates some difficulties, which Marx is aware of but brushes aside for plausible enough reasons. If, in the final analysis, all interest payments have to be furnished directly or indirectly out of surplus value, then the crucial relationship to be examined is that between interest-bearing capital and surplus value production.

The very broad definition of interest, which justifies Harvey's remark, is in Chapter 23 of Volume III (p. 502), where Marx posited:

> Interest is the net profit … yielded by property in capital as such, whether to the mere lender, who remains outside the reproduction process or to the owner who employs his capital productively himself. Yet it does not yield him this net profit in so far as he is a functioning capitalist, but rather as a money-capitalist, the lender of his own capital as interest-bearing capital to himself as functioning capitalist. Interest therefore simply expresses the fact that value in general—objectified labor in its general social form—value that assumes the form of means of production in the actual production process, confronts living labor-power as an autonomous power.

Given the level of centralization and concentration as well as the inter-twining of industrial and money capital resulting from the deep changes brought about since the late 1980s, the central antagonistic relationship is the one in which workers are placed in direct opposition to the demands of interest-bearing capital in the labor market and the workplace and as borrowers from banks. I will return to the latter dimension below.

Corporate governance

Corporate governance offers the crudest expression of the primacy of capital-as-property over capital-as-function. The formation of shareholders and managers as distinct groups dates back to the invention of the joint-stock company. Stock companies, Marx (1981: 512) observed, "have an increasing tendency to separate the work of management as a function from the ownership of capital."[9] The margin of initiative and autonomy given to industrial managers has varied considerably over the 20th century. The climax of their power was celebrated by Galbraith (1967), but in the 1990s the balance of power between industrial managers and shareholders moved sharply in favor of the former.

The issue raised by Berle and Means (1967)—namely, that "the direction of industry by persons other than those who have ventured their wealth raises the question of the motive force at the back of such direction and the effective distribution of the returns from business enterprise"—was smothered in the prosperous decades of World War II military economy and postwar reconstruction. However, it was unearthed by Jensen and Meckling (1976) and became the foundation of the contemporary theory of agency and the obligations of value to shareholders (see Lazonick and O'Sullivan 2000). The radical assessment of the current U.S. situation as set out by Lazonick (2014) is that of a transition "from value creation to value extraction." This refers not to the outsourcing of relations between large firms and their subcontractors discussed below but to the division of corporate profit to the advantage of shareholders and senior executive remunerated through stock options.

The methods used include stock buy-backs and the elaboration of strategies influencing the movement of stock prices. Lazonick (2014) calculated that between 2003 and 2012, companies in the Standard and Poor's (S&P) 500 used 54 percent of their earnings to buy back their own stock, and dividends absorbed another 37 percent. He names these strategies "stock market manipulation." Since the late 1990s, in the United States and subsequently in other advanced capitalist economies, recourse to external methods of control through the stock market has been coupled with stock option-based remuneration systems for corporate executives, aimed at creating a close common financial interest and perspective between managers and shareholders. In 2012, for the 500 highest-paid executives in proxy statements, compensation came at a rate of 42 percent in the form of stock options and 41 percent in stock awards. Lazonick saw this as a leading cause not only of "inequitable incomes," which is certainly the case, but also "of unstable employment and sagging productivity." Implicitly, his position on employment and productivity is similar to the one refuted by Williams and Kliman. Real capital formation in the United States has been affected by much deeper factors than the distribution of dividends and buy backs, pertaining notably to the issue raised by Solow (1987), "You can see the computer age everywhere but in the productivity statistics,"[10] and subsequently by Gordon (2016).

Intercorporate power relationships in the distribution of surplus value

In a context of very slow world GDP growth, the dearth of new technology with high investment requirements and profit-lifting capacity and the demands of shareholders, firms can only prosper at the expense of other firms. What becomes crucial is corporate power that affects the distribution of surplus value at each point of the circuit of capital: M–C–P–C′–M′. Mergers and acquisitions (M&As) as instruments of the centralization of capital have taken a further strategic dimension—namely, the acquisition, or now almost invariably the consolidation, of oligopolistic and monopsonistic power.[11] The share of a corporation in the distribution of surplus value will always depend in part on how cheaply it buys and exploits labor power. But otherwise its share will depend on its bargaining power vis-à-vis other firms. This starts at M, where firms experience very different conditions regarding the financing of investment from SMEs, which have to negotiate with banks to large corporations whose bond issues are eagerly waited for and snapped up by investors.

The power of retailers

When demand is very weak, the access to consumers (point C′ of the circuit) becomes particularly crucial. The economic power of the giant retailers is a trait of financialization. Up to the 1990s, the brand names built up by large U.S. corporations and European TNCs through product innovation and large advertising outlays along the Nestlé and Unilever model allowed them to negotiate with retailers in favorable conditions. Then scale and power shifted in favor of the very large global retailers: Walmart, Tesco, and Carrefour. One indicator has been the growth of the share of products under private (e.g., retailer) label. As a recent study stressed, "there are very few vendors that can compete with the global retailers in terms of scale: Walmart International alone is now bigger than Nestlé and, indeed, Walmart's annual expenditure on private label—at over $100 billion—tops Nestlé's annual revenues" (Berg and Roberts 2012: 93).

Focusing on Walmart U.S., the same study reported survey results "showing that around 120 vendors or service providers name Walmart as a major customer, on average, for 21 percent of their total sales, with the proportion reaching as high as 55 percent" (Berg and Roberts 2012: 82). Among the U.S. corporations placed high in the survey of Walmart dependency, the largest is Del Monte, the ill-famed producer of canned vegetables and fruit and pet care products operating in Mexico and Central Latin America. Not only does Del Monte sell its own brands through Walmart, it also produces Walmart's private labels.

Global value chains

For small and medium-sized firms producing specialized equipment and other material inputs to production of commodities belonging to constant capital, access to the market means selling to other firms that belong to Marx's Department I of the capitalist economy. These firms are now generally very large corporations—as in automobiles (Nissan, Renault, Volkswagen, and their first-tier suppliers)—which can dictate their terms to smaller suppliers. These can be endogenously born firms but also firms set up following the outsourcing of previous functions carried out in-house in large factories. Rather than encompassing the whole production process, large corporations started in the late-1970s to decompose the production process and resort to subcontracting, keeping for themselves the conception and design of products, as well assembly and marketing. The costs of adapting output to demand were shifted to subcontractors.

In industries such as automobiles, reduction in the size of factories also weakened trade unions. Since the early 2000s, the process straddled frontiers and came to be known under the name of global value chains (GVCs). With sophisticated information and telecommunication technologies and trade liberalization, large corporations internationalized their strategy, and global outsourcing and offshoring became central. Current business-school thinking has theorized that, "the relentless forces of com-petition and globalization are forcing firms to disaggregate and reach for foreign inputs, markets, and partners. By disaggregating their value chain into discrete pieces—some to be performed in-house, others to be out-sourced to external vendors—a company hopes to reduce overall costs and risks" (Contractor et al. 2010). While "possibly also reaping the ben-efits of ideas from their contractors or alliance partners worldwide" (Marxist terms), the corporation reaps a part of the value-added pro-duced by the subcontractors. These are forced to transfer a part of their "own" surplus value to the contractor and so to lower the wages and intensify the rhythm of work of their workers.

UNCTAD documented that in the industries where they are most used, the growth of GVCs has been outpacing that of foreign direct investment. This is the case in electronics, where major TNCs include Dell, Hewlett Packard, and Apple.

[This growth is] driven by a number of key advantages for TNCs: (a) the relatively low upfront capital expenditures required and the limited working capital needed for operation; (b) reduced risk exposure; (c) flexibility in adapting to changes in the business cycle and in demand; and (d) as a basis for externalizing non-core activities that can often be carried out at lower cost by other operators. (UNCTAD 2011: 122)

U.S., Japanese, and European firms contract local intermediaries possessing their own network of suppliers, which can be quite large, while some are TNCs in their own right. The Taiwanese corporation Foxconn operating in electronics, notably at its huge factory in Shenzhen, is the best known among them. The principals with which Foxconn works include Apple, Cisco, Dell, Microsoft, Motorola, Nintendo, Sony, Toshiba, and Nokia.

In consumer product industries, the contractors are the very big retailers, with Walmart at the fore. The corporation's CEO boasted, "by leveraging our scale and restructuring our relationship with suppliers, we will enable our businesses around the world to offer even more competitive pricing on merchandise and to provide our customers a clear and compelling assort-ment of better quality products at lower prices".[12] The full meaning of this was brought out by the catastrophes in Bangladesh: the Tazreen Fashions factory fire in November 2012, the Rana Plaza factory collapse in April 2013, and the November 2013 fire, all in Dhaka. Walmart was implicated in all three. The downstream business model is one in which an indigenous capitalist builds a factory, buys machinery, hires workers, and oversees operations in the workplace, while the U.S. or European subcontracting corporation chooses material input suppliers, provides designs, and then handles the marketing in its chain of stores.

Profits of the largest corporations

The outcome of monopoly and monopsony and of production organized along GVCs and alongside the appropriation by corporations of surplus in the form of portfolio revenue is the superior level of profits of very large corporations. A partial indicator of a higher, and indeed much higher, level of corporate profits is provided by stock-market data. In 2015, just 28 firms in the S&P 500 collectively appropriated more than half the total net income reported by U.S.-based companies in the index. In 2014, 52 S&P companies had generated half the overall corporate profit. They were headed by Apple, which reported 6.7 percent of the total net income of U.S.-based companies. A 2017 academic research paper found that big firms accounted for a larger percentage of dividend payouts and a larger percentage of total payouts in 2015 than in 1975 (see Kathleen and Stulz 2017). The top 100 dividend-paying firms accounted for 55.1 percent of total dividends in 1975. By 2015, the figure was 68.7 percent.

Contemporary banking and the sources of financial profits

Since the second half of the 1990s, the term *bank* has designated a diversified financial conglomerate, with very large insurance companies being the other form of financial conglomerate. The transformation of banking in the United States followed the emergence of pension funds as major financial actors and the growth of the corporate bond market, depriving commercial banks of part of their business and forcing them to start diversifying out of traditional activities. The process was reinforced by the steps taken by the Fed and the federal government toward liberalization and deregulation (Guttmann 1994: 263).

Banks responded by offering corporations new credit instrument: certificate of deposits (CDs). Further negotiable credit instruments were created to facilitate interbank loans, freeing banks from the constraints of having to keep large reserves of cash and very liquid securities. In their drive toward diversification, the commercial banks created mutual funds for their customers and set up hedge funds for those with a high-risk appetite and for proprietary trading. The larger commercial banks vied with the Wall Street investment banks. The growth of financial market intermediation saw the emergence of a new breed of financier: the fund manager.

In Continental Europe, liberalization and privatization took the form of the full reemergence in the 1990s of large "universal banks," which were to become highly internationalized. In many countries the process involved large mergers, and in the French case these were monitored by the government. The large E.U. banking groups offer their customers an entire range of banking and capital market services. Estimates by Pastré (2006) of returns on equity for a sample of European conglomerates ranged from 35 percent for private wealth management, 28 percent for mutualized fund management, 20 percent for investment banking, 16 percent for retail banking, and 8 percent for commercial banking.

Financial managers are subject in the same way as their industrial counterparts to the obligations of corporate governance and must satisfy the precept of value for shareholders. In the case of banking conglomerates, profitability comes from a variety of sources, among which gains from transactions in increasingly fictitious assets theorized in a banking model devised in the early 2000s. Commissions and fees in the provision of financial services—notably the financial engineering of M&As in the case of industrial corporations and the floating of bonds for governments—pertain to the category of interest as do loans to SMEs and commercial credit. But to satisfy shareholders, financial managers will need successful operations in financial markets. Loans to households require specific attention.

Interest from loans to worker households

The broader setting of this source of interest and so of financial profit is that of payments made to pension funds by workers whereby their savings are transformed into interest-bearing capital held by very powerful institutional investors, e.g. pension funds and insurance companies and their hedge fund offshoots. The relationship pertains to the point made by Marx (2010) in *Wage Labor and Capital* in relation to the first saving banks, in which,

> [T]he workers themselves give into the hands of their enemies the weapons to preserve the existing organization of society which subjugates them. The money flows back into the national bank, this lends it again to the capitalists and both share in the profits and thus ... increase their capital, their direct ruling power over the people. (Marxist.com)

In Chapter 36 of Volume III of *Capital*, Marx used the term *secondary exploitation* starting with rent paid to landlords:

> the renting of houses, etc., for individual consumption. It is plain enough that the working-class is swindled in this form too, and to an enormous extent, but this is also done by the petty trader, who supplies workers with means of subsistence. This is secondary exploitation, which proceeds alongside the original exploitation that takes place directly within the production process itself. (745)

This can be seen as the antecedent to what Lapavitsas and Dos Santos (2008) named the "historically new, *exploitative* modes of appropriation from the independently secured income of wage-earners."[13]

Today, in particular in the United States, interest and fees on mortgage, credit cards, student loans, and the like are a component of the profits of banking conglomerates The resort by workers to consumer credit has been driven by the stagnation of real wages since the 1990s and developed alongside the privatization of education and healthcare in Europe. The "withdrawal of the state" (Lapavitsas 2013) meant that access could only be secured by private means and so by borrowing. The reinstatement in the era of financialization of essentially usurious relations between banks and workers raises the question put by Norfield (2014) of the relation of "double exploitation" (secondary exploitation is preferable) to the labor theory of value. He argued that the interest paid to banks by wage earners must either represent a lowering of the value of labor power or be a deduction made by banks from the profits of productive capitalists. The first explanation is the correct one. In recent years, the lowering of the value of labor power can be seen in the rise of housing rents in a context of severe wage containment.

Gains on transactions in financial markets

A straightforward relationship, analogous in this respect to the one discussed immediately above, exists between investment banks and their customers when they charge commissions and fees for the provision of services to nonfinancial corporations and governments, such as underwriting issues of corporate and government securities, brokerage services, and the engineering of M&As. Among investors and their offshoots, as well as among investment banks in their proprietary trading, managers seek profitability essentially in the continuous reconfiguration of their portfolios and in successful speculative operations in financial markets.

Since the coming to maturity of pension funds in the mid-1970s, the course of financial accumulation and the deepening of financialization have seen the emergence of several funds. In the case of retirement schemes, this process started with the creation of defined contribution schemes as distinct from defined benefit schemes. Defined benefit pension schemes guarantee an income at retirement based on tenure with an employer as well as the wage earned. In a defined contribution scheme, benefits depend on contributions from individual scheme members, with additions from their employers in most cases, but also on stock market returns made on the sum contributed. The most widely used defined contribution scheme in the United States is the 401(K) regulated saving plan.

Next are mutual funds—namely, collective investment schemes in which the savings of many small individual investors are pooled and invested in assets, principally corporate bonds. Investors are shareholders of the fund and have a proportional claim on the returns of its investments. Mutual

funds are widely used by wage earners in many countries as a complementary or principal means to build retirement savings.

Hedge funds were first set up by industrial corporations in their currency
activities and adopted by pension funds on account of their unregulated
status to act as vehicles for high-risk speculative investments. Although all
large banks have hedge-fund-like affiliates to escape regulation and make
gains from speculation, today hedge funds are generally privately owned
investment funds. The largest funds control major industrial corporations
and collect their dividends, engage in the most highly speculative operations, and charge high fixed and performance fees. They are very selective
and open only to wealthy investors.

A recognized consultancy source on assets under management (AUM)
reported that after a short set-back in 2009, assets have continually risen,
standing at €65.7 trillion at the end of 2017, up from €26.5 trillion at the
end of 2009 (Kennedy 2018). They are held by 400 financial corporations
headed by a 12-member group managing over €1 trillion, with BlackRock,
Vanguard Group, State Street Global Advisors, and Fidelity topping €2 trillion. An unknown part of their profits is not generated by dividend and
interest as shaped by the composition of their portfolios but comes from
speculative gains. When these profits are seen from the viewpoint of productive accumulation, Hilferding's (1910: chap. 8, Marxist.com) observation
remains totally topical:

> Speculative gains or losses arise only from variations in the current valuations of
> claims to interest. They are neither profit, nor parts of surplus value. ... They are
> pure marginal gains. Whereas the capitalist class as a whole appropriates a part of
> the Labor of the proletariat without giving anything in return, speculators gain only
> from each other. One's loss is the other's gain. *"Les affaires, c'est l'argent des autres."*

Gains in the process of division and redivision of previously created surplus value can termed "fictitious profits," as by Brazilian economists
Carcanholo and Nakatani (1999) and Carcanholo and Sabadini (2008), and
by Jones (2013), or again "dubious profits" by Duménil and Lévy (2011: 8).

The originate-to-distribute banking model and shadow banking

When Hilferding wrote his book, the arena of this zero-sum-game was the
stock-market. From the early 2000s onward, however, it became that of an
extremely complicated web of financial markets and trading transactions
stemming from the originate-to-distribute banking model and lodged in
the shadow banking system. A Federal Reserve Bank of New York staff
paper by Bord and Santos (2012: 21) defined the originate-to-distribute
banking model as a method that "enables banks to remove loans from balance sheets and transfer the credit risk associated with those loans. It

involves selling the loans to a third party (the loan originator and the borrower being the first two parties)."

Traditionally, loans remained on the asset side of balance sheets and were identifiable. Securitized loans are taken off the balance sheet and sold to other banks or funds, which sell the assets to other investors. Banks set up affiliates with the U.S. legal form of trusts, named "special investment vehicles" or "special purpose vehicles" (SIVs and SPVs). These were charged with pooling assets that were worthless separately as corroborated by the need to pool them in high risk financial instruments which rating agencies rated positively allowing them to be sold to investors. Mortgage-backed securities (MBS) and asset-backed securities (ABS) were the most frequent assets of this type. Traders named this "offloading" or "risk-stripping." Paulani (2010) spoke of processes in which "the most degenerated forms of financial assets seem to be the source of their own increase."

The shadow banking system results from the extension of the originate-to-distribute intermediation model throughout the financial system.[14] It is officially defined by the Financial Stability Board (2011: 1) as "a system of credit intermediation that involves entities and activities outside the regular banking system, and raises (a) systemic risk concerns, in particular by maturity/liquidity transformation, leverage and flawed credit risk transfer, and/or (b) regulatory arbitrage concerns."[15] These "entities" include non-bank mortgage lenders offering no income and no asset housing loans, SPVs, and SPEs set up by banks and hedge funds. Through their affiliates, Wall Street conglomerates combining retail and investment banking activities and European "universal banks" joined the system.

Another Federal Reserve of New York staff paper (Adrian and Ashcraft 2012: 2), stressed that the "operations of many shadow banking vehicles and activities are symbiotically intertwined with traditional banking and insurance institutions." The Financial Stability Board (FSB) admitted that "the risks in the shadow banking system can easily spill over into the regular banking system" and that they "are amplified as the chain becomes longer and less transparent" (FSB 2011). This is what occurred in 2008, when the shadow banking system provided the terrain for very rapid systemic contagion. Yet it has not only survived the crisis but, in 2012, it started to grow anew.

Oligopolistic market rigging and investor swindling

The tight oligopoly formed by the small group of large banks has created the conditions for collusion and market rigging. A major example of this was the concerted rigging in 2008 of the key international financial instrument, the London Interbank Offered Rate (LIBOR) benchmark interest rate for interbank overnight loans, for which Barclays, UBS, RBS, Deutsche Bank, JP Morgan, Citigroup, and Bank of America were investigated and fined. The collusion provoked great indignation, but the banks had the power to smother it. Charges of swindling investors were made against major individual banks in the wake of 2008, as in the case of the New York Securities Commission's charge against Goldman Sachs for "defrauding investors by misstating and omitting key facts about a financial product tied to subprime mortgages as the housing market was beginning to falter" and against Citigroup's principal U.S. broker-dealer subsidiary for "misleading investors about a $1 billion CDO tied to the housing market" (Security and Exchange Commission 2016). Later, the U.S. subsidiary of UBS was fined for not warning the Central and Western Corporate credit unions about the risks of $1.15 billion of residential MBS bought in 2006 and 2007 (Stempel 2017).

Looking ahead

After a short setback in 2009, claims on present and future surplus value first continued to grow faster than its production and appropriation before reaching a plateau and receding a bit in developing economies (not in developed mature capitalist countries). Even if it has dropped slightly, the amount of money-capital seeking is huge. In 2016, the Bank for International Settlements (BIS) coined the term "appetite for risk" to characterize the behavior of investors. A more explicit term, that of "yield-hungry," has replaced it. Financial profits are hard to gain. The outcomes are the unabated intensity of trading and the recourse to high-risk assets. The Fed considers cautiously that the mechanisms that led to the 2008 crisis have been dismantled by the banks themselves and by regulation.[16] But the October 2018 International Monetary Fund (2018) *Global Financial Stability Report* lists an impressive number of "near-term risks." The authors of a note posted on the IMF blog observed that, "With interest rates extremely low for years and with ample money flowing though the financial system, yield-hungry investors are tolerating ever-higher levels of risk and betting on financial instruments that, in less speculative times, they might sensibly shun" (Adrian, Natalucci, and Piontek 2018).

The IMF staff sees the global market for "leveraged loans," estimated to be around $1.3 trillion, as a point in the financial system at which a new crisis could start. These are loans arranged by a syndicate of banks to firms heavily indebted or with weak credit ratings. Underwriting standards and credit quality have deteriorated. In the United States, new deals include fewer investor protections (covenants) and lower loss-absorption capacity. Institutions hold about $1.1 trillion of leveraged loans in the United States, almost double the precrisis level. Some $1.2 trillion in high-yield bonds is outstanding, the principal one being collateralized loan obligations (CLOs) issued by financial corporations, including the affiliates of major banks, which package small loans and sell them to investors as for the precrisis MBS and ABS.[17]

Mutual funds investing in leveraged loans have grown from roughly $20 billion in assets in 2006 to about $200 billion in 2018, while "institutional ownership makes it hard for banking regulators to address potential risk to the financial system if things go wrong."(Adrian, Natalucci, and Piontek 2018) McKinsey Global Institute (2018: 8) reported that in the United States almost 40 percent of all nonfinancial corporate bonds are now rated BBB, just a few steps above noninvestment grade. Furthermore, the average credit quality of investment-grade borrowers has declined, issuance having been particularly strong in bonds that are below investment grade: speculative-grade or high-yield bonds.

Although the debt of the developed economies has receded, that of developing countries has grown considerably, from 20 percent in 2004–2007 to 60 percent of total world debt in 2016 (Mbaye and Moreno Badia 2019). Today, the other point of potential high financial vulnerability are the investments made by funds in the corporate bond markets of a number of developing countries. Cross-border investment flows into these bonds demonstrate significant volatility, reflecting the risks associated with them due weak governance and management, and less transparency on corporate financial performance. The large amount of debt issued in foreign currencies adds another layer of risk in the case of some companies. If the local exchange rate depreciates, the cost of servicing foreign currency debt rises, increasing the possibility of default. Many corporate issuers in developing economies have fragile finances relative to the size of their current debt-service payments. McKinsey Global Institute (2018:18) estimated that up to 25 percent of corporate bonds in developing countries are at risk of default.

Investors might be taught that risk should be "sensibly shunned"; if they did not know that, after reaching a certain size, they would be protected by the theory and policy of the "too big to fail."[18] For the history of financial accumulation is such that, since the bail out of the Continental Illinois bank in 1984, bail outs have become the rule. The failure of Lehmann Brothers in 2008 is the exception that proves the rule and took place because of the absolute need to bail out American Insurance Group (AIG) on account of its systemic centrality.[19] The global perspective is that of the slow world GDP growth and the risk of a major global financial crisis. Such is today the assessment of financialization.

Notes

1. I am aware of the controversies around the status of Volume III of *Capital*, and of Part 5 in particular. But this does not affect the extreme importance of the theoretical avenues Marx opened up in those chapters.

2. Despite a fall in 2008–2009, the combined global debt of governments, nonfinancial corporations, and households has grown by $72 trillion since the end of 2007. The advanced and emerging market economies' nonfinancial sector debt now amounts to some 225 percent of world GDP. The increase is smaller but still pronounced when measured relative to world GDP. However, there has been a retrenchment in private debt buildup among advanced economies. It is marginally on the rise but well below its peak (see Mbaye and Moreno Badia 2019).

3. Marx emphasised, "this collection of small amounts, as a particular function of the banking system, must be distinguished from the banks' functions as middlemen between actual money capitalists and borrowers."

4. Duménil and Lévy 2011 spent a lot of energy trying to present them as strong pillars of effective demand.

5. These were calculated by McKinsey Global Institute, even if the estimates only have the status of a proxy as market valuations were used for their calculation. They grew at a compound annual average rate of 9 percent from 1990 to 2007, with a sharp acceleration in 2006 and 2007 (+18 percent). That year the ratio of financial assets to world GDP rose to 359 percent (McKinsey Global Institute 2009). The 20-year period of strong growth was brought to a halt by the 2007–2008 financial crisis. Due to soaring public debt following the government rescue of the major banks in the United States and Europe in 2008, and again in Europe in 2012, global financial assets in 2013 surpassed their precrisis totals, even if McKinsey regretted that "growth has hit a plateau and slowed to an anemic 1.9 percent since the crisis" (McKinsey Global Institute 2013).

6. Sweezy (1994) wrote: "This theory is best described, I think, as an "overaccumulation" theory. It holds that under monopoly capitalism as it has developed in the advanced capitalist countries during the twentieth century there is a strong, persistent, and growing tendency for more surplus value to be produced than can find profitable investment outlets. … the result will be a decline—or slowdown in the rate of growth—of output and income, with rising unemployment and falling rates of utilization of productive capacity. And this situation in turn puts an added damper on investment and economic growth." (Sweezy 1994: 42)

7. Duménil and Lévy (2011: 153) argued that the rate of accumulation is closely related to the "level of retained profits," what is left to managers once interest and dividends are paid. Later in the book, when they offered their expertise to U.S. policymakers, one point concerning the need to "invert neo-liberal trends towards dis-accumulation" (Duménil and Lévy 2011: 301).

8. These are all appropriations of surplus value and appear as "profits without production" *only* at the level of the individual firm. The problem is that Krippner's term was subsequently used by some Marxists to characterize contemporary capitalism more broadly.

9. Indeed, the "capitalist mode of production has brought matters to a point where the work of superintendence, entirely divorced from the ownership of capital, is always readily obtainable" (Marx 1981: Chap. 23, p. 511).

10. For an enlightening update on U.S., productivity, see Smith (2018).

11. According to UNCTAD (2014), following the "shift to services," international M&A operations reached a peak around 2004–2006. Estimates published in a recent official U.S. study indicated that global activity in mergers and acquisitions surpassed $5 trillion in 2015, about $2.5 trillion of which was in the United States, "the highest amount in a year on record." Deals surpassing $10 billion accounted for 37 percent of global takeovers in 2015, almost double the average of 21 percent for the previous five years (Economic Report of the President 2016). The process has pursued since. In 2018, "Rising global trade tensions did not manage to stifle acquisitions: Deals involving companies based in different countries accounted for more than 40 percent of all announced transactions" (Grocer 2018).

12. http://www.storebrandsdecisions.com/news/2010/02/02/wal-mart-creates-global-mercha ndising-centers-to-streamline-sourcing

13. An interesting historical account is given by Bellofiore and Halevi (2010).

14. In this model, "the four key aspects of intermediation are 1° maturity transformation: obtaining short-term funds to invest in longer-term assets; 2° liquidity transformation: using cash-like liabilities to buy harder-to-sell assets such as loans; 3° leverage: employing techniques such as borrowing money to buy fixed assets to magnify the potential gains (or losses) on an investment; 4° credit risk transfer: taking the risk of a borrower's default and transferring it from the originator of the loan to another party" (Kodres 2013: 1-2).

15. The board almost apologized for using the term: "some authorities or market participants prefer to use other terms such as "market-based financing" instead of "shadow banking." It is important to note the use of the term "shadow banking" is not intended to cast a pejorative tone on this system of credit intermediation. However, the FSB has chosen to use the term as this is most commonly employed and has been used in the earlier G20 communications" (Financial Stability Board (2011: 1).

16. "Banking institutions have built stronger capital and liquidity buffers that, together with reforms to the rules governing money market funds, strengthen the ability of institutions to withstand adverse shocks and reduce their susceptibility to destabilizing runs. Recovery and resolution plans have helped ensure that risks leading to the failure of financial intermediaries are borne by the institutions and investors taking the risks and not U.S. taxpayers" (Board of Governors of the Federal Research System 2018).

17. https://www.ft.com/ … /db97c650-1ec6-11e9-b126-46fc3ad87c65

18. Bernanke defined the term in 2010: "A too-big-to-fail firm is one whose size, complexity, interconnectedness, and critical functions are such that, should the firm go unexpectedly into liquidation, the rest of the financial system and the economy would face severe adverse consequences."

   He continued, "Governments provide support to too-big-to-fail firms in a crisis not out of favoritism or particular concern for the management, owners, or creditors of the firm, but because they recognize that the consequences for the broader economy of allowing a disorderly failure greatly outweigh the costs of avoiding the failure. If the crisis has a single lesson, it is that the too-big-to-fail problem must be solved." (Bernanke 2010: 1)

19. A March 15, 2019, financial newsletter returns to the event: "AIG's swaps on subprime mortgages pushed the company to the brink of bankruptcy. As the mortgages tied to the swaps defaulted, AIG was forced to raise millions of dollars in capital. As stockholders got wind of the situation, they sold their shares, making it

even more difficult for AIG to cover the swaps. AIG was so large that its demise would have impacted the entire global financial system. The $3.6 trillion money-market fund industry had invested in AIG securities. Most mutual funds owned AIG stock. Financial institutions around the world were also major holders of AIG's debt" (Amadeo 2019).

References

Adrian, T., and A. Ashcraft. 2012. "Shadow Banking Regulation." Federal Reserve Bank of New York Reports, 559, April.

Adrian, T., F. Natalucci, and T. Piontek. 2018. "Sounding the Alarm on Leveraged Lending." IMF Blog. https://blogs.imf.org/2018/11/15/sounding-the-alarm-on-leveraged-lending/

Amadeo, K. 2019. "AIG bailout, cost, timeline, bonuses, effects." The Balance. https://www.thebalance.com/aig-bailout-cost-timeline-bonuses-causes-effects-3305693

Berg, N., and B. Roberts. 2012. *Walmart: Key Insights and Practical Lessons from the World's Largest Retailer.*, London, UL: Kogan Page.

Berle, A., and G. Means. 1967. *The Modern Corporation and Private Property.*, 2nd edition, New York, NY: Harcourt, Brace and World.

Bellofiore, R., and J. Halevi. 2010. "Magdoff-Sweezy, Minsky and the Real Subsumption of Labour to Finance." Available at https://www.researchgate.net/publication/304637518_Magdoff-Sweezy_Minsky_and_the_Real_Subsumption_of_Labour_to_Finance

Board of Governors of the Federal Reserve System. 2018. *Financial Stability Report.* https://www.federalreserve.gov/publications/files/financial-stability-report-201811.pdf

Bord, V., and J. Santos. 2012. "The Rise of the Originate-to-Distribute Model and the Role of Banks in Financial Intermediation", *Economic Policy Review* 18 (2): 21–33.

Carcanholo, R., and P. Nakatani. 1999. "O capital especulativo parasitário: uma precisão teórica sobre o capital financeiro, característico da globalização", *Ensaios FEE, Porto Alegre*, 20(1): 284–304.

Carcanholo, R., and M. Sabadini. 2008. "'Capital Ficticio y Ganancias Ficticias', Herriamenta, 37", http://www.herramienta.com.ar/revista-herramienta-n-37/capital-ficticio-y-ganancias-ficticias>.

Chesnais, F. 2016. Finance Capital Today. *Corporations and Banks in the Lasting Global Slump*. Chicago: Haymarket Books.

Chesnais, F. 2019. "De nouveau sur l'impasse économique historique du capitalisme mondial." https://alencontre.org/economie/de-nouveau-sur-limpasse-economique-historique-du-capitalisme-mondial.html

Contractor, Farok, V. Kumar, S. Kundu, and T. Pedersen. 2010. "Reconceptualizing the Firm in a World of Outsourcing and Offshoring: The Organizational and Geographical Relocation of High-Value Company Functions." *Journal of Management Studies* 47(8): 1417–1433.

De Brunhoff, S. 2004. "Marx's Contribution to the Search for a Theory of Money", In *Marx's Theory of Money: Modern Appraisals*, edited by Fred Moseley. London, UK: Palgrave Macmillan.

Duménil, G., and D. Lévy. 2011. *The Crisis of Neoliberalism*. Cambridge, MA: Harvard University Press.

Financial Stability Board 2011., Shadow Banking: Strengthening Oversight and Regulation, Recommendations of the Financial Stability Board, 27 October. https://www.fsb.org/wp-content/uploads/r_111027a.pdf?page_moved=1

Galbraith, J. 1967. *The New Industrial State.* Princeton, NJ: Princeton University Press.

Gordon, R. 2016. *The Rise and Fall of American Growth: The U.S. Standard of Living since the Civil War.* Princeton, NJ: Princeton University Press.

Grocer, S. 2018. "A Record $2.5 Trillion in Mergers Were Announced in the First Half of 2018." *New York Times.* https://www.nytimes.com/2018/07/03/business/dealbook/mergers-record-levels.html

Guttmann, R. 1994. *How Credit-Money Shapes the Economy: The US in a Global System.,* New York, NY: M.E. Sharpe, Amonk.

Hanieh, A. 2012. "Finance, Oil and the Arab Uprisings: The Global Crisis and the Gulf States." *Socialist Register* 48:176–99.

Harvey, D. 1982. *Limits to Capital.* Oxford, UK: Basil Blackwell.

Helleiner, E. 1994. *States and the Reemergence of Global Finance: From Bretton Woods to the 1990s.* Ithaca, NY: Cornell University Press.

Hilferding, R. 1910. "Finance Capital." Available at: https://www.marxists.org/Archive/Hilferding/1910/Finkap/.

International Monetary Fund. 2018. *Global Financial Stability Report.* Available at: https://www.imf.org/~/media/Files/Publications/GFSR/2018/Oct/CH1/doc/text.ashx?

Jensen, M., and W. Meckling. 1976. "Theory of the Firm: Managerial Behavior, Agency Costs and Ownership Structure." *Journal of Financial Economics* 3(4): 305–360.

Jones, P. 2013. "The falling rate of profit explains falling US growth." Available at https://thenextrecession.files.wordpress.com/2013/12/jones-the-falling-rate-of-profit-explains-falling-us-growth-v2.pdf

Kathleen, K., and R. Stulz. 2017. "Is the US Public Corporation in Trouble?" *Journal of Economic Perspectives* 31(3): 67-88. doi: 10.1257/jep.31.3.67.

Kennedy, L. 2018. "Top 400 Asset Managers 2018: 10 Years of Asset Growth." *IPE Reference Hub.* https://www.ipe.com/reports/special-reports/top-400-asset-managers/top-400-asset-managers-2018-10-years-of-asset-growth/10025004.article

Kliman, A. 2012. *The Failure of Capitalist Production: Underlying Causes of the Great Recession.,* London, UK: Pluto Press.

Kodres, L. 2013. "What Is Shadow Banking." *Finance and Development, IMF* 50(2): 42–43.

Konings, M. 2010. "Beyond the Re-regulation Agenda", *In the Great Credit Crash*, edited by M. Konings. London, UK: Verso.

Krippner, G. 2005. "The Financialization of the American Economy." *Socio-Economic Review* 3(2):173–208. vol. doi: 10.1093/SER/mwi008.

Lapavitsas, C., and P. Dos Santos. 2008. "Globalisation and Contemporary Banking." In Contributions to Political Economy, vol. 27, 31-66.

Lapavitsas, C. 2013. *Profiting without Production: How Finance Exploits US All.* London, UK: Verso.

Lazonick, W. 2014. "Profits without Prosperity." *Harvard Business Review*, September,

Lazonick, William, and Mary O'Sullivan. 2000. "Maximizing Shareholder Value: A New Ideology for Corporate Governance." *Economy and Society* 29(1):13–35. doi: 10.1080/030851400360541.

Marx, K. 2010. "Wage Labour and Capital, Markup: Zodiac and Brian Baggin." Available at https://www.marxists.org/archive/marx/works/1847/wage-labour/index.htm

Marx, K. 1978. *Capital.* Vol. II, London, UK: Pelican Books.

Marx, K. 1981. *Capital.* Vol. III, London, UK: Pelican Books.

Mbaye, S., and M. Moreno Badia (2019). "New Data on Global Debt." *IMF Blog.* https://blogs.imf.org/2019/01/02/new-data-on-global-debt/

McKinsey Global Institute 2009. Global Capital Markets: Entering a New Era, September. https://www.mckinsey.com/~/media/McKinsey/Industries/Private%20Equity%20and%20 Principal%20Investors/Our%20Insights/Global%20capital%20markets%20entering%20a %20new%20era/MGI_Global_capital_markets_Entering_a_new_era_gcm_sixth_annual_ full_report.ashx

McKinsey Global Institute 2013. Financial Globalization: Retreat or Reset?, March. https:// www.mckinsey.com/featured-insights/employment-and-growth/financial-globalization

McKinsey Global Institute 2018. 'Rising Corporate Debt: Peril or Promise?', Discussion Paper, June. https://www.mckinsey.com/business-functions/strategy-and-corporate-finan ce/our-insights/rising-corporate-debt-peril-or-promise

Norfield, T. 2014. "Capitalist Production Good, Capitalist Finance Bad." Available at: http://www.economicsofimperialism.blogspot.co.uk/2014/01/

Pastré, O. 2006. Les restructurations bancaires européennes : bilan et perspectives. Conseil Scientifique de l'AMF, Février.

Paulani, L. 2010. "The Autonomization of Truly Social Forms in Marx's Theory: Comments on Money in Contemporary Capitalism", Paper presented at Sixth International Marx Congress, Nanterre. Available at: http://www.jourdan.ens.fr/levy/ dle2010.pdf.

Roberts, M. 2018. "Financialisation or profitability?" https://thenextrecession.wordpress. com/ November 27.

Security and Exchange Commission. 2016. "SEC enforcement actions: Addressing miscon- duct that led to or arose from the financial crisis." http://www.sec.gov/spotlight/enf- actions-fc.shtml

Smith, N. 2018. "Maybe We Have the Economic-Growth Equation Backward." *Bloomberg*. https://www.bloomberg.com/opinion/articles/2018-12-04/maybe-we-have-the-economic- growth-equation-backward

Solow R. 1987. "We'd better watch out." *New York Times* Book Review, July 12, page 36.

Stempel, J. 2017. "UBS Pays $445 Million Over Toxic Mortgages and Failed US credit Unions." *Business Insider France*. http://www.businessinsider.fr/us/ubs-mortgage-settle- ment-2017-5

Sweezy, P. 1984. "Some problems in the theory of capital accumulation." In *The Faltering Economy*, edited by J.B. Foster and Henryk Szlaifer, 41–56. New York, NY: Monthly Review Press.

UNCTAD 2011. World Investment Report, Geneva, June.

UNCTAD 2014. World Investment Report, Geneva, June.

Williams, S., and A. Kliman. 2014. Available at https://blogs.lse.ac.uk/usappblog/2014/10/ 09/falling-profits-rather-than-increasing-financial-investment-led-to-decreasing-rates-of- capital-accumulation-by-american-companies/

State involvement in cryptocurrencies. A potential world money?

Juan J. Duque

ABSTRACT

This article is about the role that states play in the research and development of cryptocurrencies and their underlying technology. Some states, for instance China, are about to launch their own state-backed cryptocurrency perhaps due to the potential of this new type of digital money to become world money. To support this argument, Marxist monetary theory is deployed to show that cryptocurrencies could be conceived as potential digital commodity money, a new and incorporeal type of commodity money with intrinsic value but without use value. Lacking a natural form, it could potentially have only a "formal" use value: direct exchangeability with all other commodities. If states manage to actualise this potential by issuing their own cryptocurrencies and making them legal tender money, cryptocurrencies could function as international means of payments and means of hoarding perhaps more efficiently than credit money. In the case of China, this means that this new digital money would have a chance of competing with the US dollar as international reserve currency.

Introduction

Cryptofinance is a new field within the economy that emerged with the invention of a decentralized software functioning as a digital double-entry bookkeeping system, namely blockchain technology (or, more accurately, distributed ledger technology, DLT). This technology appeared in theoretical form in 2008 in a paper signed by an unknown author(s) called Satoshi Nakamoto, and was launched in January 2009, when the open-source software analyzed in Nakamoto's text was actually developed. Bitcoin was created in the form of a working-as-a-currency data, the first data to be introduced in a blockchain.

Blockchain-based DLT systems are programed as a chain of blocks where new data additions are initiated by one of the nodes, thus creating a new block and sharing it with all the network, which then conclude its validity in function of a pre-defined algorithmic validation method, adding it to the ledgers of the nodes (World Bank 2017, 2). Distributed networks can also be programed in other ways without this block dynamic[1]. Nevertheless, and due to the fame of the initial example, many authors talk about block-chain when their ideas could often be applied to any type of DLT. In the rest of the paper, I will use the term "DLT/blockchain".

Cryptofinance can be defined as a field that includes transactions, institutions and social relations in general around all kinds of financial data introduced in a DLT/blockchain. Within cryptofinance, cryptocurrencies are the original and most famous innovation, comprising new digital currencies that, thanks mainly to cryptography, can guarantee trust without the need of a third party, simply through their own software. DLT/blockchain technology has more uses, both in the field of finance and outside it. Other sectors in which the technology has been used, or is being considered for use, are accounting, insurance, administration, and several others involving data sharing. Social scientists have also paid attention to DLT/blockchain and cryptocurrencies, especially economists (for instance, Ciaian, Rajcaniova, and Kancs 2016; Hendrickson, Hogan, and Luther 2016; Casey et al., 2017; Makarov and Schoar 2020). There are also philosophical approaches to these issues (e.g., Bjerg 2016; Velasco 2017; Dos Santos 2017; Chainiyom and Giordano 2019), as well as major institutions that have produced related research (for instance, UK Government Chief Scientific Adviser 2016; World Bank 2017). Moreover, there are "financial gurus" and advisors of all kinds, and even a current of economic thought around this technology, the "institutional cryptoeconomics" (Berg, Davidson and Potts 2017; Davidson, de Filippi and Potts 2018). Thus, not surprisingly, central banks and other state institutions have also started to pay attention to this technological innovation.

With the rise of cryptofinance in the private sector, central banks and transnational financial institutions started to undertake research on how to apply these innovations from the standpoint of the public sector. The results are several reports on Central Bank Digital Currency (CBDC) or Central Bank Crypto Currency (CBCC) (for example, Bech and Garratt 2017; Sveriges Riksbank 2017, 2018; Norges Bank 2018; Bank of Israel 2018; Mancini Griffoli et al. 2018; European Central Bank 2019; Boar, Holden, and Wadsworth 2020; Auer and Böhme 2020). Some pilot projects exist in countries like Ecuador and Uruguay, and China plans to issue a legal tender cryptocurrency in the near future. Cryptofinance becomes an example of a monetary and financial innovation that emerged in the private sector and started to be assimilated and adopted by the state. The argument put forth in this paper is that states are increasingly involved in cryptocurrencies in large part because these currencies have the potential to become international reserve currency (i.e. a form of world money).

World money is the form of money that adequately fulfills the functions of means of international payments and means of hoarding in the world market, the "universal wealth" (Marx 1990 [1867], 242). Historically, gold has been the world money. It is proposed in this paper that cryptocurrencies are a new type of digital money with the potential to become a sort of "digital gold". A key reason why states such as China are about to launch their own state-backed cryptocurrency is to strengthen their ability to compete with the US dollar as (quasi) world money in the contemporary world market[2].

This paper is organized as follows: first, the qualitative differences between digital monies are explained, introducing cryptocurrencies as a new type of digital money and discussing some of the innovations carried out by several financial institutions, mainly central banks. Second, the analytical content of cryptocurrencies is examined by relying on Marxist monetary theory, and particularly the idea of money's "formal" use value, which helps characterize cryptocurrencies as potential digital commodity money. Third, the relation between an increasingly multipolar global monetary and financial system and DLT/blockchain is considered in some detail. Fourth, the case of China is developed, focusing on the relationship of the Chinese state to Bitcoin and the design of a CBCC that is expected to be launched. The last section concludes.

Digital money and institutional research on cryptofinance

The first step is to examine the differences between distinct types of digital (or electronic) money. Digital money is not something new, as money has been digitalized for decades. What is new are cryptocurrencies. That is why I will use "CBCC" (Central Bank Crypto Currency) and not "CBDC" (Central Bank Digital Currency) to refer to the legal tender cryptocurrencies that are being designed and developed. Credit money is already digitalized, so the differentiating characteristic of CBCC is not its digital, but its "crypto" character[3].

Lapavitsas (2013, 87–100) divides digital money into access e-money and e-money proper. Access e-money, the electronic form of credit money, is the most widespread type of digital money, being "[...] an envelope term that captures several means of transferring conventional credit money electronically" (Lapavitsas 2013, 93). It is basically an electronic transfer of credit money, the main form of money worldwide. Its extension was mainly due to the digital revolution and the technological change that followed, with the subsequent transformation of the banking sector. Some examples of access e-money are credit and debit cards, credit transfers, direct debits, etc. The other form of e-money, more recent than access e-money and closely related to the development of financialization, is e-money proper. It is privately issued money stored on electronic devices and purchased with ordinary money at par value. Some examples are "[…] prepaid cards, or prepaid software programmes used on the internet, often called server-based e-money" (Lapavitsas 2013, 97), which are frequently issued by industrial and commercial enterprises of developing countries, where the financial system is weak.

Cryptocurrencies are a third type of e-money, the most recent form, and completely different from the others. It is not a liability that returns to the issuer when loans mature and are repaid, so it is not credit money. It is also not a liability of an issuer that is bought at par by advancing another form of money (credit or fiat). Finally, it is not an inconvertible and valueless symbol issued by the state to replace commodity money, so it is not fiat money. Instead, it can be thought of as a special type of commodity money: (potential) digital commodity money. This will be explained in further detail in the next section using Marxist monetary theory[4].

Bech and Garratt (2017, 55–70), in a report for the Bank for International Settlements, characterized CBCC as money that is issued by the central bank, electronic, universally accessible, and enabling payment with no intermediary through a peer-to-peer network. CBCC could replace not only cash, but also bank deposits, or part of them. As it is very safe and liquid, it could compete with (or substitute) private banks' credit money. Obviously, its final impact depends on how it is introduced. The degree of substitution of bank deposits by CBCC will depend on how this new money is configured and implemented. For example, the People's Bank of China is considering a "double level system", where the existing financial system uses the new money: CBCC should focus on the replacement of M0 (i.e. cash and banks' deposits in the central bank), without charging interest and maintaining the financial intermediation of commercial banks.

For Christine Lagarde (2018), the central bank should function only as the DLT/blockchain platform, as a protocol for monetary transactions, thus improving financial inclusion, security and consumer protection, as well as privacy in payments. Auer and Böhme (2020) classify Central Bank *Digital* Currencies primarily in regard to the banking architecture in which they operate: indirect (private banks' intermediation), direct (central bank handling wholesale and retail payments) or hybrid (private banks' intermediation but with central bank periodically recording retail balances). Following from this, they look if the digital currency is a centralized ledger, or based on a DLT/blockchain. Within the latter, they in turn classify the

CBCC as requiring identification (accounts-based) or not (token-based). As it has been said, this article is only concerned with the second type, the DLT/blockchain-based digital currencies, which can be designed and introduced in many ways.

The central banks that are seriously considering launching a CBCC are thinking of doing it without structurally modifying their national credit systems. This obliges them to maintain the intermediation of private banks, keeping their credit money. However, a future is conceivable that allows CBCCs to replace private banks' credit money, dramatically changing formal financial systems. Regardless of how CBCCs are introduced, the implications of introducing this new type of digital money should be understood from a political economy perspective. Thus, understanding the potential global changes in capitalism that cryptocurrencies can bring, and why states are moving in.

Political economy of cryptocurrencies

Cryptocurrencies are a new type of digital money that uses a DLT/blockchain, electronic money that uses a database containing all the transactions ever executed in a peer-to-peer network (Atzori 2017, 45–46). The crucial characteristic is that consensus between the users of this database can be easily achieved thanks to cryptographic algorithms that validate and record transactions, without the need of knowing or trusting each other.

There are different types of DLT/blockchains, and thus different types of cryptocurrencies. One way to classify them is by the cryptographic algorithm chosen to ensure the proper functioning of the software. The exact function that cryptography performs is guaranteeing a very high resistance to fraud and counterfeiting, preventing the software from being hacked[5]. The most famous example of cryptographic algorithm is Bitcoin-like proof-of-work, but there are others: proof-of-consensus (Schwartz, Noah, and Britto 2014), different types of proof-of-work algorithms (Cheng et al. 2018), proof-of stake (Chohan 2018), and others like proof-of-research or proof-of-authority. Some of these options have already been developed and others are only designed, but the point is that there are lot of feasible alternatives, even hybrid algorithms. It requires a high degree of technical knowledge to think about how to use cryptography to design and code an algorithm able to generate consensus in a DLT/blockchain. In the case of cryptocurrencies, depending on their cryptographic algorithm they can be mined or not. This means that they are either created through rewards to the "miners" that solve complex mathematical problems using hardware and electricity, or they are created in other ways. Mining new cryptocurrencies is characteristic of those that use the proof-of-work algorithm, with miners fulfilling the function of validating new transactions and recording them to the ledger. Mineable cryptocurrencies can also be pre-mined to a greater or lesser degree, i.e. the creators of the cryptocurrency produce a certain number of units before it can be mined.

Another way to classify DLTs/blockchains (and cryptocurrencies) is differentiating among them on the basis of whether they are permissionless or permissioned. This basically amounts to whether anyone or only approved people can run a node. But the distributed nature of the ledger, and the fact that there is no trusted third party as cryptography guarantees security, does not mean that there cannot be a DLT/blockchain in which an authority decides who enters the network and makes changes to the ledger. In fact, this can be companies, public institutions, or groups of people who create their own DLT/blockchain and decide who can and cannot participate, depending on certain parameters. In contrast to a centralized ledger, the ledger of a permissioned DLT/blockchain does not need a central authority to ensure that the information it contains continues to function in a safe and reliable way.

The main point about the essence of cryptocurrencies is that it does not matter who is enabled to make changes in the ledger (whether permissionless or permissioned), nor what cryptographic algorithm they use to guarantee security (which implies that they can be minable cryptocurrencies or not), but simply that they are peer-to-peer networks that use cryptography so that they can be trusted simply through its own software. In the case of a permissioned (or private) cryptocurrency, the centralized nature of states and central banks and the distributed nature of DLTs/blockchains are perfectly compatible.

Formal use value

For Karl Marx (1990 [1867], 125–137), commodities have use value, their usefulness arising from the concrete labor, and value, the abstract (socially necessary) labor they contain, which is reflected as exchange value when several commodities are considered. Theoretically, money arises as a result of the dialectic between two moments of the expression of value that occur in exchange and that relate commodities to each other: the relative form, the expression of the value of a commodity in another commodity, and the equivalent form, its immediate interchangeability for other commodity as potential material to express the value of it (Marx 1990 [1867], 138–163).

There is one type of commodity which has evolve in exchange with other commodities differently, being increasingly accepted as the equivalent in which the rest expresses their value, and finally adopting the money form. These are the "money-commodities", those that end with their natural form (their use value) and their equivalent form (their capacity to serve as material for the expression of value) socially intertwined. Historically, commodities such as precious metals, mainly gold, have mostly been the ones that have managed to become the general equivalent, i.e. money. Cryptocurrencies are potential digital commodity money, so we ought to consider their integration into the theory. To do so, "formal" use value must be examined.

Marx (1990 [1867], 183–184) explains formal use value as an additional use value that money-commodities acquire. For him:

> The money commodity acquires a dual use-value. Alongside its special use-value as a commodity (gold, for instance, serves to fill hollow teeth, it forms the raw material for luxury articles, etc.) it acquires a formal use-value, arising out of its specific social function. (Marx 1990 [1867], 184)

The "specific social function" is to be the universal equivalent, the capacity of expressing the value of any commodity. So, apart from its use value as the raw material for luxury objects, gold has direct exchangeability with all other commodities, its formal use value. Cryptocurrencies are a very special type of commodity money: they are digital, lacking a natural form. Thus, they have no use value that could compare to gold's usefulness as a metal, but only a potential formal use value. They are an incorporeal commodity comprising digital information created through coding whose materiality is certainly related to the digital world (in the infrastructures of the Internet, in the electronic devices, and in the "digital abstraction" of bits from physical media to binary information[6]). There is no use value in cryptocurrencies, only a potential formal use value that could only be actualized if the dialectic of the expression of value evolved properly into the money form as cryptocurrencies were deployed. For this dialectic to end in the appearance of money, both certain physical characteristics of the money-commodity ("homogeneity, durability, divisibility and so on") and social custom are needed (Lapavitsas 2005, 567). In potential digital commodity money, the special physical characteristics that are required for a commodity to reach the money form are not given by nature. Instead, these are socially-programed, with social custom being the most complex and difficult factor to materialize. Contrary to what happens with precious metals, there is no social habit or tradition associated with their separate use value to facilitate cryptocurrencies evolving into the money form.

Digital commodity money

Cryptocurrencies are potential digital commodity money, a digital commodity that is designed and produced with the only purpose of becoming money. Digital commodity money has no natural form but, similarly to gold and all other commodities, its production starts from the free gifts of nature and human nature. Marx, speaking about fixed capital, stated that:

> Nature builds no machines, no locomotives, railways, self-acting mules, etc. These are products of human industry; natural material transformed into organs of the human will over nature, or of human participation in nature. They are *organs of the human brain, created by the human hand*; the power of knowledge, objectified. The development of fixed capital indicates to what degree general social knowledge has become a *direct force of production*, and to what degree, hence, the conditions of the process of social life itself have come under the control of the general intellect and been transformed in accordance with it. (Marx 1993 [1939], 706. In Italics in the original).

In the case of precious metals, the fixed capital involved in production is the machinery and infrastructures required for gold and silver mining, which in turn encapsulates the "general social knowledge" involved in their design and production. Just as with the mining industry, the production of digital commodity money has its own fixed capital. There is a great amount of knowledge objectified in the global infrastructures that compose the Internet, in the electrical grids and in the digital devices required for the development and production of the software that makes digital commodity money. Energy consumption is another crucial factor in understanding the digital world's materiality, and the abstract labor encapsulated in digital commodity money. The energy use is dependent on the cryptographic algorithm chosen in the design and production of the corresponding cryptocurrency.

It is in the sphere of exchange that the money-commodity (digital or not) truly reaches the money form. Thus, the vital difference between money-commodities is apparent: while precious metals have a natural form, cryptocurrencies do not. This means that, while in the first case there is a corporeal commodity with use value (such as being the material for jewelry and other luxury items) that goes into the market and reaches the money form, in the second there is just a digital (and thus incorporeal) commodity with no use value, whose only purpose is to become money. If cryptocurrencies adequately reach the money form, the intrinsic value of the ability to buy would be produced without any provided-by-nature and useful-for-something matter as the natural form of the money-commodity. It would only be a digital commodity with software coded into a kind of "socially-programmed natural form", but without a natural form in the strict sense of the term. It has no use value. Its only purpose would be to attain the money form, thus reaching directly the last stages of Marx's evolution of the expression of value. If the last stage (the money stage) is reached in market exchange through the actions of commodity owners, thus also acquiring the requisite social custom, the cryptocurrency would actualize its potential formal use value: it would have direct exchangeability with all other commodities.

Monetary and financial multipolarism, and DLT/blockchain technology

Contemporary money is mainly digitalized credit money[7]. It is basically credit money issued by private banks backed by central bank money, a peculiar hybrid of fiat and credit money issued by the bank of banks (Lapavitsas 2013, 82–87). But not all credit monies have the same weight in the world market. There is a particularly important one, used for most international payments: the US dollar, the (quasi) world money. Basically, "[w]orld money serves as the universal means of payment, as the universal means of purchase, and as the absolute materialization of wealth as such (universal wealth)" (Marx 1990 [1867], 242). The world market is not culturally or legally homogeneous, and it does not have an integrated credit system that coordinates it. World money is the world market's organizer by serving as a means of hoarding and payments for international capitals and states, apart from a common measure of value and an instrument for inter-state political and military power (Lapavitsas 2013, 101–105). In the current world, the US dollar functions as a coordinator of world trade and finance, and the military power of the USA as guarantor of stability and good functioning.

Military and financial hegemony are closely related. Yet, despite the USA having substantial advantages, such as military bases across the globe, maritime control, use of the US dollar by other central banks in their international reserves, the most important banks and financial centers, and globally influential monetary policy, the hegemonic position of the USA has been challenged by China and other states for some time (de Brunhoff 2009 [2006], 50–59). In recent years, this growing multipolarism has become more acute, and Russia and Iran have openly confronted US hegemony alongside China. Finance, in this respect, has become a crucial geopolitical instrument.

The Society for Worldwide Interbank Financial Telecommunication (SWIFT) is a not-for-profit institution that offers its services as a payments network to banks and other financial institutions from all around the world. SWIFT's protocol software had become "[...] a de facto sector technology standard" (Scott and Zachariadis 2012, 475), being the trusted third party for global financial transactions, the communication channel of financial institutions. Officially, SWIFT is an independent institution headquartered in Belgium, but it is Western-controlled. Within the West, it is the USA that has the greatest control over SWIFT. This could be clearly seen when President Trump withdrew the USA from the Iran nuclear deal and imposed financial restrictions on dealing with Iran, despite the objections of the European allies of the USA. Germany, France and the United Kingdom looked for ways to overcome the restrictions that the USA imposed unilaterally due to its financial hegemony. Then, in 2018, by order of the USA, SWIFT disconnected the Iranian banks from the organization that controls global financial communications[8]. Europe tried and failed to avoid the US restrictions, but developed INSTEX, a non-US dollar and non-SWIFT special purpose vehicle designed to support transactions with Iran (for humanitarian purposes).

In this increasingly multipolar world, China and Russia are designing and developing alternatives to SWIFT. Chinese Cross-Border Interbank Payment System (CIPS) and Russian financial messaging system SPFS[9] are planned to be integrated, thus having an embryonic payment and financial communications system, capable of competing with SWIFT at a global level. For this project to succeed, it is relevant to note that DLT/blockchain technology would be important.

Developing and pioneering DLT/blockchain technology in finance can make a big difference when creating a system that competes with SWIFT and a (quasi) world money that competes with the US dollar. The potential of this monetary and financial innovation was quickly perceived by countries opposed to US hegemony[10], with China in the lead. Cryptocurrencies could potentially function as world money more easily than credit money. Further, a payment mechanism employing a a DLT/blockchain software could be more reliable globally.

Money with intrinsic value functions more adequately as means of hoarding and means of international payments, and functions more adequately as world money (the "universal wealth"). The US dollar, a value-less type of money, is a currency which does not require any link with commodity money to operate as world money[11], being the international reserve currency due to the hegemonic status of the USA. This is an important reason why countries like China and Russia are very interested in DLT/blockchain.

China

Since Bitcoin appeared in 2009, China has been watching closely, actively participating in projects and actions related to cryptofinance. It has reached a point where it is likely to be the first country to issue a CBCC, and that would be a major step in the development of cryptocurrencies.

Bitcoin

Although it may never properly function as money, Bitcoin is potential digital commodity money, a monetary innovation that interested the

Chinese authorities from the very beginning. Kaiser, Jurado, and Ledger (2018) explain the evolution of Bitcoin in China, concluding that the Asian country is a great danger due to its ability and motivations to hack the cryptocurrency. They show some types of possible attacks and state that China has enough capacity to carry them out because of its advantageous position in the Bitcoin ecosystem and its control of the domestic economy and technology (Kaiser, Jurado, and Ledger 2018, 15). While they perhaps exaggerate the danger posed by China, their analysis summarizes perfectly the evolution of the relationship between the Chinese authorities and the Bitcoin community.

According to these authors, Bitcoin was introduced and promoted in 2013 due to several factors, including: the growth in private wealth, the favorable foreign exchange rate for the Yuan, the familiarity of the Chinese people with online and mobile payment systems (e.g. mobile wallet apps), and the possibility of circumventing government control and censorship (Kaiser, Jurado, and Ledger 2018, 16–17). The authors show that, from 2013 to 2017, China dominated the exchange volume of Bitcoin. In December 2013 the Chinese government enacted laws against money laundering, prohibiting banks from treating Bitcoin as a currency, so Bitcoin exchanges started using alternative financial systems instead of banks, exploiting regulation loopholes. Exchanges were allowed to continue with their activities as long as they identified their clients and obeyed the new regulation. They evidently found workarounds to continue with their business, causing the Yuan to dominate worldwide Bitcoin exchange activities. Then, in early 2017, regulators started banning ICOs[12] and, in September, the exchanges were closed. "Loopholes such as over-the-counter sales, peer-to-peer trading, and foreign listings were banned in early 2018 forcing exchanges to finally abandon the Chinese market and relocate. As a result, Chinese exchanges now accounts for less than 1%" (Kaiser, Jurado, and Ledger 2018, 17).

The history of Bitcoin mining in China is quite different. This activity not only was not restricted since 2013 but was actually promoted. Local governments offered tax incentives and energy and land discounts to mining companies, which were organized in pools. A pool is a group of miners who collaborate and can be located anywhere in the world. It is the location of the managers that places the pool geographically. Managers located in China came to control 50 percent of total Bitcoin network hash power in 2015, exceeding this percentage since 2016. On Bitcoin mining, Kaiser, Jurado, and Ledger (2018, 17–18) explain that, apart from cheap land and electricity in Chinese regions such as Sichuan and Inner Mongolia, there is also the advantage for miners of having easy accessibility to the electronic chips required for the work (made-in-China Application-Specific Integrated Circuits). These factors pushed China to the fore in terms of processing power for Bitcoin mining. But, at the beginning of 2018, the Chinese government ordered local regulators to stop the preferential policies for Bitcoin mining companies. Regulators were told to alter policies previously supportive of miners (basically electricity pricing, taxes, and land use) to dissuade them from continuing their work. The official reasons were mainly due to energy use, but the action coincided with the country's serious regulation of cryptofinance. Despite this development, China remains the country whose pool managers control the greatest amount of hash power.

China's CBCC

The People's Bank of China began researching a prospective CBCC since cryptocurrencies emerged. The most concrete details of the project have been kept secret from the beginning, although its general outline has become known. China is going to test the so-called "digital currency electronic payment" (DC/EP) in some selected cities. A project that has been postponed, among other reasons, due to the coronavirus pandemic.

Early 2018, Fan Yifey, the vice-president of the People's Bank of China, publicly considered a "double level system" where the existing financial system would use a new type of digital money, a legal tender cryptocurrency[13]. The CBCC should focus on the replacement of M0 (cash and banks' deposits in the central bank), without charging interest, while maintaining the financial intermediation of commercial banks. In this way, the introduction of a CBCC would not have a major impact on the functioning of the existing monetary and financial system, or of the productive sector.

Regarding the two crucial factors for a money-commodity to achieve the money form (certain physical characteristics and social custom), China's future legal tender cryptocurrency is going in the right direction. Similarly to all previous cryptocurrencies, China's CBCC is designed and will be produced with the physical characteristics required to become money. This means that, in contrast to non-digital commodity money, cryptocurrencies do not have a natural form with naturally-given quantities and attributes, so the rules must be coded in the software. Therefore, the quantity that will exist, the ways in which this quantity will change, the manner in which it will be obtained by users, and even the ways in which the rules themselves could be changed, will be known in advance and permanently. This would make cryptocurrencies acquire a sort of "socially-programmed natural form", but without strictly having a natural form (since they would still have no use value but only a potential formal use value). In the case of China, the appropriate government institutions would choose the blockchain/DLT and its rules. The result would be a legal tender digital currency composed by a permissioned (state-controlled) blockchain/DLT.

However, apart from having ideal physical characteristics to monopolize direct exchangeability, social custom would also be necessary. It is probable that China's CBCC is going to be the first cryptocurrency that will fully achieve the money form by acquiring the required social custom by law. Obviously, the fact that the Chinese people are already used to online and mobile payments, with apps such as WeChat and Alipay, will contribute to achieving the social custom. Regarding the stability of value that this new type of legal tender money will have, this has to be studied more in depth. In the introduction to this special issue about digital-community currencies and cryptocurrencies ("Good Money Drives Out Bad"), Makoto Nishibe speaks about the stability of different types of money. If money is classified between "bad" and "good", it seems that CBCCs will be better money than credit money in terms of value (they have intrinsic value) but worse than precious metals, being necessary to study how stability will evolve. An important point to be considered is the random path proper of commodity money, that CBCCs are going to follow, in comparison with credit money's circular path[14].

Conclusion

DLT/blockchain is a decentralized software that functions as a digital double-entry bookkeeping system, a database that contains all the transactions ever executed in a peer-to-peer network of which the security and validity is guaranteed thanks to cryptographic algorithms. Cryptocurrencies are a new type of digital money that uses this technology, avoiding being hacked simply through its own software. In this way cryptocurrencies are able to achieve consensus between the users without the need of a trusted third party.

Since they appeared in 2009 with Bitcoin, cryptocurrencies started to arouse a lot of interest among national governments. They are a new type of digital money, different from digitalized credit money and from privately-issued digital money purchased with ordinary money at par value like prepaid cards or software programs. Cryptofinance appeared in private exchange, quickly attracting the attention of states. Many financial institutions, mainly central banks, started researching the possibility of issuing a CBCC. They produced reports proposing different ways of introducing a CBCC as a complementary type of money to the national credit system, without structurally modifying the latter.

Cryptocurrencies (i.e. working-as-a-currency data introduced in DLTs/blockchains) have different cryptographic algorithms to generate consensus among users. Depending on which algorithm they deploy, they could be mineable or not. Cryptocurrencies (or, more accurately, DLTs/blockchains) could also be classified as permissionless (public) or permissioned (private), basically reflecting whether anyone or only approved people could run a node of the DLT/blockchain. They are a decentralized software with a peer-to-peer network and cryptographic algorithms that could also have an authority to decide who enters the network and makes changes to the ledger. The difference with a non-DLT/blockchain, centralized data-sharing system is that a permissioned DLT/blockchain could continue to exist and be trusted even if there was not such authority.

This new type of digital money was analyzed in this paper from the perspective of Marxist monetary theory as a recent and special type of potential money-commodity. It is an incorporeal commodity with no natural form, and thus with no use value, but only a potential formal use value, namely direct exchangeability with all other commodities. Cryptocurrencies are thus potential digital commodity money. However, despite being designed and produced to become money, most cryptocurrencies fail to do so. The fundamental reason is that they require certain physical characteristics and social custom (the difficult factor to achieve) attached to them successfully to reach the money form.

In the contemporary world market, the US dollar functions as (quasi) world money, i.e. the means of international payments and hoarding, thus being the international reserve currency. This legal tender credit money is the organizer of the world market, supporting a form of financial hegemony that is sustained by the military and political hegemony of the USA. Thus, the SWIFT payments mechanism among financial institutions is also controlled by the USA. It is a not-for-profit institution whose protocol software has been established as the standard for communications between banks and other financial institutions all around the world. It is notable that China and Russia are preparing alternatives to SWIFT. Along similar lines, China is gradually preparing to launch its own CBCC. The new international payments mechanism and China's CBCC are going to use DLT/blockchain, and they have the opportunity to succeed as the nature of hegemony changes across the world.

The Chinese state is aware of the potential of cryptocurrencies to become world money, and has thus acted as a pioneer in the research and development of a CBCC. Given that cryptocurrencies already have programed in them the key physical characteristics required for a commodity to reach the money form, it might well be the case that the Chinese CBCC would be the first instance of a cryptocurrency acquiring the missing element, namely: social custom. The reason for that would be state involvement in its issuing, but also the already extensive acquaintance of the Chinese people with online and mobile payments.

Notes

1. Some examples of non-blockchain DLTs, like the software of the cryptocurrency IOTA and the one of the open-source distributed ledger platform Corda, can be found here: https://medium.com/blockstreethq/before-blockchain-there-was-distributed-ledger-technology-319d0295f011.

2. The term "quasi world money" was originally deployed by Makoto Itoh to describe central banks' credit money competing to be world money (Lapavitsas 2013, 104).

3. It should be borne in mind that in some existing literature, both academic and non-academic, the term "digital currencies" is used to refer to the DLT/blockchain-based, legal tender currencies that are being researched and/or developed by institutions such as central banks. In other words, to refer to cryptocurrencies, specifically permissioned ones issued by central banks.

4. There are several contemporary authors who have addressed the field of economics through the ideas of Marx, many of them focusing especially on finance and monetary issues. Some examples are de Brunhoff 2015 [1976]; Weeks 1981; Harvey 2018 [1982]; Foley 1986; Itoh 1988; Itoh and Lapavitsas 1999; Saad-Filho 2002; Fine and Saad-Filho 2016 [2004]; Patnaik 2009; Lapavitsas 2013.

5. Cryptography avoids the double spending problem in a digital currency, i.e. the hacking of the software to use many times the same units of the currency, or other kinds of attacks. In the digital world, the double spending problem is particularly difficult to solve without an intermediary, because digital currencies are ultimately series of digits in a string of binary code (Zimmer 2017, 311). Thus, Bitcoin's big innovation is that it is a decentralized digital currency that solves this problem through cryptography, being able to be trusted just through its own software, and guaranteeing its safe and proper functioning.

6. To read more about the "digital abstraction" and the materiality of the digital world, see Blanchette (2011a, 2011b).

7. Although gold has never ceased to have a role as the original money commodity that is increasingly hoarded in times of crisis.

8. In 2012 SWIFT had already been used to sanction Iran, but it is in 2019 when Iranian banks are completely disconnected by order of the USA.

9. SPFS system was created in 2014 to protect Russia from a potential disconnection of SWIFT. This happened when Barack Obama's administration, after imposing different types of international sanctions to Russia due to the conflict in Ukraine, was thinking of expelling Russian banks from the SWIFT system. At that moment, Russian authorities decided to create SPFS just in case the disconnection was carried out.

10. A failed example of this is the Petro, the cryptocurrency that the Venezuelan government created in 2018 trying to overcome the commercial and financial sanctions that the USA has been imposing on the Latin American country, and as a desperate solution to try to refloat an economy that is sinking.

11. In 1971, Richard Nixon suspended direct convertibility of US dollar to gold, which was already unnecessary.

12. An Initial Coin Offering is the creation and sale of a new cryptocurrency. This is the official statement of the People's Bank of China banning ICOs, in Chinese: http://www.pbc.gov.cn/goutongjiaoliu/113456/113469/3374222/index.html

13. This is the double level system proposal of Fan Yifey, in Chinese: https://www.yicai.com/news/5395409.html

14. More about the path that money follows depending on its type in Lapavitsas (1991).

References

Atzori, Marcella. 2017. "Blockchain Technology and Decentralized Governance: Is the State Still Necessary?" *Journal of Governance and Regulation* 6 (1):45–62. doi:10.22495/jgr_v6_i1_p5.

Auer, Raphael, and Rainer Böhme. 2020. "The Technology of Retail Central Bank Digital Currency." In *Bank for International Settlements Quarterly Review*, 85–100.

Bank of Israel. 2018. "Report of the Team to Examine the Issue of Central Bank Digital Currencies." Bank of Israel, November 2018.

Bech, Morten, and Rodney Garratt. 2017. "Central Bank Cryptocurrencies." In *Bank for International Settlements Quarterly Review*, 55–70.

Berg, Chris, Sinclair Davidson, and Jason Potts. 2017. "The Blockchain Economy: A Beginner's Guide to Institutional Cryptoeconomics." *Medium*.

Bjerg, Ole. 2016. "How is Bitcoin Money?" *Theory Culture & Society* 33 (1):53–72. doi:10.1177/0263276415619015.

Blanchette, Jean-François. 2011a. "A Material History of Bits." *Journal of the American Society for Information Science and Technology* 62 (6):1042–1057. doi:10.1002/asi.21542.

Blanchette, Jean-François. 2011b. "The Noise in the Archive: Oblivion in the Age of Total Recall." In *Computers, Privacy and Data Protection: An Element of Choice*, edited by Serge Gutwirth, Yves Poullet, Paul De Hert and Ronald Leenes. Heidelberg: Springer, 25–38.

Boar, Codruta, Henry Holden, and Amber Wadsworth. 2020. "Impending Arrival – A Sequel to the Survey on Central Bank Digital Currency", *BIS Papers No. 107*.

Casey, Michael, Jonah Crane, Gary Gensler, Simon Johnson, and Neha Narula. 2017. "The Impact of Blockchain Technology on Finance. A Catalyst for Change." Geneva Reports on the World Economy, Vol. 21. International Center for Monetary and Banking Studies (ICMB).

Chainiyom, Siwittra, and John Giordano. 2019. "On Bitcoin and Simmel's Idea of Perfect Money." *Prajñā Vihāra* 20 (1):52–65.

Cheng, Zhuan, Gang Wu, Hao Wu, Muxing Zhao, Liang Zhao, and Qingfeng Cai. 2018. "A New Hybrid Consensus Protocol: Deterministic Proof of Work". Accessed April 24, 2019. https://www.google.com/url?sa=t&rct=j&q=&esrc=s&source=web&cd=4&ved=2ahUKEwiimsOVxujhAhXBRxUIHcqlDfcQFjADegQIAxAC&url=https%3A%2F%2Farxiv.org%2Fpdf%2F1808.04142&usg=AOvVaw1xynpUTJrrSHSm9wauF-Gg.

Chohan, Usman W. 2018. "Proof-of-Stake Algorithmic Methods: A Comparative Summary." Discussion Paper Series: Notes on the 21st Century, University of New South Wales, Canberra. School of Business and Economics.

Ciaian, Pavel, Miroslava Rajcaniova, and d'Artis Kancs. 2016. "The Economics of Bitcoin Price Formation." *Applied Economics* 48 (19):1799–1815. doi:10.1080/00036846.2015.1109038.

Davidson, Sinclair, Primavera de Filippi, and Jason Potts. 2018. "Blockchains and the Economic Institutions of Capitalism." *Journal of Institutional Economics* 14 (4) :639–658. doi:10.1017/S1744137417000200.

de Brunhoff, Suzanne. 2009 [2006]. "Finanzas, Capital, Estados." In *Las Finanzas Capitalistas: Para Comprender la Crisis Mundial*, edited by François Chesnais, Suzanne de Brunhoff, Gérard Duménil, Michel Husson and Dominique Lévy. Buenos Aires: Herramienta, 25–78.

de Brunhoff, Suzanne. 2015 [1976]. *Marx on Money*. London: Verso.

Dos Santos, Renato P. 2017. "On the Philosophy of Bitcoin/Blockchain Technology. Is It a Chaotic." *Metaphilosophy* 48 (5):620–633. doi:10.1111/meta.12266.

European Central Bank 2019. "Exploring anonymity in central bank digital currencies", *InFocus. Issue no. 4.*

Fine, Ben, and Alfredo Saad-Filho. 2004 [2016]. *Marx's Capital.* 6th ed. London: Pluto Press.

Foley, Duncan K. 1986. *Understanding Capital. Marx's Economic Theory.* Cambridge (US): Harvard University Press.

Harvey, David. 2018 [1982]. *The Limits to Capital.* London: Verso.

Hendrickson, Joshua R., Thomas L. Hogan, and William J. Luther. 2016. "The Political Economy of Bitcoin." *Economic Inquiry* 54 (2):925–939. doi:10.1111/ecin.12291.

Itoh, Makoto. 1988. *The Basic Theory of Capitalism. The Forms and Substance of the Capitalist Economy.* London: Palgrave Macmillan.

Itoh, Makoto, and Costas Lapavitsas. 1999. *Political Economy of Money and Finance.* London: Palgrave Macmillan.

Kaiser, Ben, Mireya Jurado, and Alex Ledger. 2018. "The Looming Threat of China. An Analysis of Chinese Influence on Bitcoin." Accessed May 15, 2019. https://www.google.com/url?sa=t&rct=j&q=&esrc=s&source=web&cd=2&ved=2ahUKEwj6o5iJw53iAhU RVRUIHaMhDEkQFjABegQIBBAC&url=https%3A%2F%2Fblockchain.princeton.edu%2Fpapers%2F2018-10-ben-kaiser.pdf&usg=AOvVaw2Ylll8Ipu5RWkxoK4r4Zf7.

Lagarde, Christine. 2018. "Winds of Change: The Case for New Digital Currency", Conference at the Singapore Fintech Festival, November 14, 2018. Accessed March 23, 2020. https://www.imf.org/en/News/Articles/2018/11/13/sp111418-winds-of-change-the-case-for-new-digital-currency.

Lapavitsas, Costas. 1991. "The Theory of Credit Money: A Structural Analysis." *Science & Society* 55 (3):291–322.

Lapavitsas, Costas. 2005. "The Emergence of Money in Commodity Exchange, or Money as Monopolist of the Ability to Buy." *Review of Political Economy* 17 (4):549–569. doi:10.1080/09538250500252823.

Lapavitsas, Costas. 2013. *Profiting without Producing. How Finance Exploits Us All.* London: Verso.

Makarov, Igor, and Antoinette Schoar. 2020. "Trading and Arbitrage in Cryptocurrency Markets." *Journal of Financial Economics* 135 (2):293–319. doi:10.1016/j.jfineco.2019.07.001.

Mancini Griffoli, Tommaso, Maria Martinez Peria, Itai Agur, Anil Ari, John Kiff, Adina Popescu, and Celine Rochon. 2018. "Casting Light on Central Bank Digital Currency." *Staff Discussion Notes* 18 (8):1. doi:10.5089/9781484384572.006.

Marx, Karl. 1990 [1867]. *Capital.* vol. I. London: Penguin Books.

Marx, Karl. 1993 [1939]. *Grundrisse.* London: Penguin Books.

Norges Bank. 2018. "Central Bank Digital Currencies", *Norges Bank Papers NO 1 | 2018.*

Patnaik, Prabhat. 2009. *The Value of Money.* New York: Columbia University Press.

Saad-Filho, Alfredo. 2002. *The Value of Marx. Political Economy for Contemporary Capitalism.* London: Routledge.

Schwartz, David, Youngs Noah, and Arthur Britto. 2014. "The Ripple Protocol Consensus Algorithm." Ripple Labs Inc 2014.

Scott, Susan V., and Markos Zachariadis. 2012. "Origins and Development of SWIFT, 1973–2009." *Business History* 54 (3):462–482. doi:10.1080/00076791.2011.638502.

Sveriges Riksbank. 2017. "The Riksbank's e-krona project. Report 1", *Sveriges Riksbank.* September 2017.

Sveriges Riksbank. 2018. "The Riksbank's e-krona project. Report 2", *Sveriges Riksbank.* October 2018.

UK Government Chief Scientific Adviser 2016. "Distributed Ledger Technology. Beyond Blockchain", *Government Office for Science.*

Velasco, Pablo R. 2017. "Computing Ledgers and the Political Ontology of the Blockchain." *Metaphilosophy* 48 (5):712–726. doi:10.1111/meta.12274.

Weeks, John. 1981. *Capital and Exploitation.* Princeton: Princeton University Press.

World Bank. 2017. "Distribute Ledger Technology (DLT) and Blockchain", *FinTech Note No. 1.*

Zimmer, Zac. 2017. "Bitcoin and Potosí Silver: Historical Perspectives on Cryptocurrency." *Technology and Culture* 58 (2):307–334. doi:10.1353/tech.2017.0038.

Index

Note: *Italicized* numbers indicate figures, **bold** indicate tables and those followed by 'n' indicate endnotes.

For Product Safety Concerns and Information please contact our
EU representative GPSR@taylorandfrancis.com Taylor & Francis
Verlag GmbH, Kaufingerstraße 24, 80331 München, Germany